LONDON COUNTRY
in the 1970s

STEVE FENNELL

Ian Allan
PUBLISHING

The new order in the South East area from July 1971 was the SM. Ordered in LT days and built to LT specification, 138 of these Swifts commenced delivery from April 1970, the vast majority being used for RT replacement. SM502 is seen outside Dartford garage one Sunday in July 1974. *Steve Fennell*

Front cover:
St Peters Street in St Albans plays host to Lincoln-green liveried RMC1513 on route 330A. RMCs replaced St Albans' last RTs in March 1972, this particular vehicle being transferred in from Addlestone following the OMO conversion of Green Line 716/A. Initially these redundant RMCs merely had the waistband painted canary yellow and GREEN LINE fleetnames replaced by LONDON COUNTRY, the paintwork within the area of the fleetname bearing testimony to this alteration. The 330 comprised one of many routes which succumbed to the economies of one-man operation during 1977, receiving new Leyland Nationals in November. *Steve Fennell*

Back cover:
May 1972 finds brand-new ANs 35, 29, 23 and 25 stored at Guildford garage in readiness for the OMO conversion of route 408 the following month. The buses carry the interim livery introduced by London Country: a shade referred to as 'mid green', with canary-yellow relief — a scheme that, sadly, was all too short-lived. *Steve Fennell*

Title page:
Throughout much of the 1970s London Country would suffer chronic vehicle shortages, caused by the unreliability of the newer types inherited from LT. Here RF170 takes on a load at Garston Queen's School in September 1973, covering for a non-existent Merlin on route 335. The vehicle also carries a somewhat illegible destination blind, produced by Norbury Bros. Such blinds were made of thinner material than the LT-produced items, allowing further destinations to be carried, but the visual quality was appalling, and thankfully few garages received such blinds. *Steve Fennell*

Contents

First Published 2003

ISBN 0 7110 2886 9

Published by Ian Allan Publishing

an imprint of Ian Allan Publishing Ltd, Hersham, Surrey KT12 4RG. Printed by Ian Allan Printing Ltd, Hersham, Surrey KT12 4RG.

Code: 0301/B3

Foreword

EVEN prior to 1970, bus operations in what was then London Transport's Country Area held considerable fascination. Aside from the fact that the London Transport name could be seen in such diverse locations as Aylesbury, Harlow and Crawley, the same high standard of operation and presentation which was so familiar in the Home Metropolis was present for all to see throughout the Home Counties. Living in South West London at the time, I recall my earliest visits into 'green bus' territory and the subsequent surprise I experienced at the discovery of the seemingly wanton mixing of vehicle types on the same route. Where one was so used to the rigidity of the Central bus operation (where even the use of a Routemaster on an RT route was considered unusual), the 'green' fleet appeared to flout such methods of operation, such was the variety on offer. At the time, of course, I failed to realise the reasoning behind such diversity and couldn't really understand the logic behind mixed crew/OMO operation on the same route. It was only some years later, with a greater understanding of the Country Bus Department's methods of working, that the economies that such variety could bring were fully appreciated. Nevertheless, the impressions gained at the time developed into a profound interest in the mixed fortunes of the Country Bus operation — so much so that my still growing Country Bus photographic collection now outnumbers my Central collection by as much as 20-1!

My earliest forays into the Country Area were in 1968. London Transport was on the verge of embarking on 'Reshaping', and vast quantities of new AEC Merlins (*née* Swifts) were stockpiled awaiting entry into service. The latter was somewhat protracted, however, due to inevitable differences of opinion between management and unions, and, despite the first production Merlins being delivered in October 1967, it was not until the following March (with one exception) that the initial examples entered revenue-earning service, from Reigate garage on route 447 (Redhill–Batts Hill–Reigate–Meadvale–Redhill–Merstham). My first ever visit, therefore, to one of LT's Country garages was to Reigate soon after their introduction. This wasn't my first visit into Country territory, however, as, thanks to family connections at Guildford, green RLHs (and maroon Tillingbourne Valley GSs) had already been discovered. Both these events helped shape an interest in the Country fleet that conspired to take up much of my spare time until the late 1970s. By then the LT influence had faded to such an extent that, to all intents and purposes, London Country (as the erstwhile Country Area was now called) had become 'just another NBC operator', which indeed was always the intention. I still made odd visits to Country Bus territory, but these were much reduced, compared with earlier in the decade. By this time my own interests were concentrated on the rapidly dwindling pockets of Routemaster operation, and, when RMC1512 operated for the last time from Swanley garage in March 1980, my attention inevitably turned to pastures new.

Prior to the infamous split of 1970 I had managed to visit nearly all of London Transport's Country garages, courtesy of the various different Rover tickets on offer at the time. Week-Ender tickets, I recall, were exceptional value, allowing travel for two days on anything with LONDON TRANSPORT on the side, including Green Line coaches. Thus, with an early start thanks to the Metropolitan Line reaching Amersham, one could be in the heart of Country Bus territory before breakfast time. Many fascinating expeditions were undertaken during these early years, and much of interest was observed. I well remember a trek to Tring to see the unique XMB15, which habituated route 387, whilst in the South East the last GS at Northfleet was sampled unknowingly just a few days before its withdrawal and replacement by one of the ubiquitous RFs.

Come 1 January 1970 and, initially at least, very little appeared to change. Inevitably the well-used Week-Ender tickets passed into history, being replaced some months later by London Country's own Golden Rover, which allowed travel both on Country buses and on Green Line coaches — but not, initially, on route 727! The newly titled London Country Bus Services still felt very much an LT operation, and at the outset the only visible changes were the appearance of gold LONDON COUNTRY fleetnames on vehicles and the new styling on publicity material. By the close of the decade, however, very little evidence of LT influence would remain.

During the second half of the 1960s London Transport had commenced a programme of operating economies brought about by the inevitable decline in public-transport usage for which the decade is now remembered. In the case of the Country Department, a considerable number of services had seen OMO conversion on Sundays, mainly using RF-class AEC Regal IVs but in some cases new AEC Merlins. These latter, 108 in total, had allowed a number of daily OMO conversions to occur in 1968/9. Other conversions utilised RFs, a number of which were surplus to requirements thanks to the aforementioned service reductions, whilst the entire single-deck Green Line network was now OMO. It was apparent, moreover, that this trend would continue under the new regime. Indeed, London Transport had ordered a total of 138 new AEC Swifts for the Country Area, and this order was inherited by London Country, with delivery commencing in May 1970. It is tempting to speculate as to what would have happened to the Country Bus operation had it remained under London Transport control. An inkling of future vehicle policy was outlined in the volume *Reshaping London's Buses*, published by Capital Transport in 1982. At one time it was intended that a total of 460 front-entrance/rear-engined Routemasters (FRMs) should provide the means for RT replacement — certainly an interesting option. As it was, the FRM project died in its infancy, so speculation must revolve around the concept of Lincoln-green Fleetlines. Indeed, the new Swifts on order were earmarked by LT for RF replacement, and, again, one can only speculate as to their intended sphere of operation.

Traditionally the headquarters of London Transport's Country fleet was at Reigate. Indeed, the original buildings used by the East Surrey Traction Co still provided accommodation for a handful of staff, and this persisted into London Country days — it was logical that the nerve centre of the new company should carry on using the buildings occupied under London Transport auspices. In the past, many functions of the administration side of the Country Department had been undertaken by London Transport, and although the new company would have to be self-sufficient, it was appreciated that this couldn't simply happen overnight. The 1930s-built LT Country Bus HQ in Lesbourne Road was incapable of accommodating all the personnel that made up the London Country empire, and thus an extension to the original building was commissioned and opened in March 1972, bringing together all Head Office staff at a single site. Despite this abundance of new office space, some staff were still housed in the original East Surrey building on the corner of Bell Street and Lesbourne Road, and this continued for a number of years.

In LT days the initial delivery of any new vehicle type for the Country Area was inevitably received at Reigate garage, and this practice continued into the London Country era — although, as the decade progressed, the appeal of such new vehicles tended to decrease. Nevertheless, it was still quite impressive to see brand-new buses awaiting entry into service, even if the vast majority were Leyland Nationals. I was employed by London Country at Reigate from March 1974 until January 1978, doing stints in Traffic Planning (planning for decline?) and Public Relations (passenger complaints!). It was certainly an interesting period in London Country's history, and my job allowed me access to information regarding vehicle workings and advance planning proposals. On reflection it was possibly not the best career opportunity of my life, but it seemed like a good idea at the time!

As can probably be deduced from the above, my own interest in the London Country story is in the era from inception until the close of crew operation, and this is the period which I have chosen as the subject for this volume. I make no apology for this emphasis on the decline of crew operation; any such work must surely reflect one's own personal interest, and I readily confess that I had very little enthusiasm for the events of subsequent years (although they would in themselves make an interesting tale!). Thus, if you are expecting the majority of illustrations to feature Atlanteans, Bristols or Nationals, then this is not the book for you. If, however, you have an affiliation with RTs, RFs, Routemasters, Merlins and Swifts — not to mention the early London Country influence — then hopefully you will find much of interest within. For those who remember the Country Bus network of the 1970s, this book should evoke memories of a time that we all took so much for granted. I also realise that, for many, the early London Country era will simply be a period of history in a relatively recent past which one may not have had the fortune to have witnessed. Either way, I hope that the story will give an impression of the atmosphere and nature of the operations of the London Country network.

I should like to thank the many people who have assisted with the compilation of this volume, particularly the many photographers who have trawled their photographic collections to provide suitable material. I should also like to acknowledge the use of the publications of the London Omnibus Traction Society, particularly its monthly newsletter *The London Bus*, which has been an extremely valuable source of information. For anyone wishing to broaden his/her knowledge of London Country, I can thoroughly recommend the volume *London Country* published recently by Capital Transport.

Steve Fennell
Didcot, October 2002

In the early 1970s a number of long-established routes fell victim to intransigence on the part of local councils. One such was the 364, which linked Hitchin with Luton and Flamstead Village, the service being withdrawn completely in July 1973. Just a few days before the end, RF625 is seen at Hitchin, commencing its long cross-country journey to Flamstead Village. *Steve Fennell*

Setting the Scene

1 JANUARY 1970 is an extremely significant date in the history of London Transport. From this time, the 1,267 vehicles that made up the operational fleet of London Transport's Country Bus & Coach Department were transferred to London Country Bus Services Ltd, a newly created subsidiary of the state-owned National Bus Company.

Even in LT days, passenger numbers had been falling at an alarming rate. The effects of ever-increasing car ownership, combined with the increased traffic congestion that inevitably arose from such a situation, conspired to make bus journeys ponderous and unpredictable. Coupled with staff shortages and fare increases, it is not hard to see that the newly formed company faced an uphill struggle from day one. Of the fleet inherited from LT, an extremely high proportion consisted of vehicles suitable only for crew operation, and the average age of the fleet as a whole was very high. Indeed, Godstone garage possessed no one-man-operated (OMO) vehicles at all, while many others had allocations comprising only RF and RT types. Prior to the split, LT had earmarked a total of 138 new AEC Swifts for the Country Area, and these orders were passed on to London Country. These new Swifts were used for OMO conversions, whilst a small batch enabled service expansion at Crawley. An early pronouncement was that of the quest for eventual 100% one-person operation, and to this end an order was placed for 90 Leyland Atlanteans and 90 AEC Reliances, both types featuring Park Royal bodywork. The Atlanteans were intended for OMO conversion of busy crew routes, whilst the Reliances were to permit the wholesale OMO conversion of the Green Line network. Together with the impending Swifts, these orders represented 318 new vehicles, and in contemporary press announcements much play was made of this fact and also of the need for continued fleet modernisation. Further vehicles earmarked were another 36 Swifts, 30 Atlanteans and 11 Daimler Fleetlines — all diverted orders from other NBC subsidiaries — bringing the total of new vehicles on order to 395.

The styling of practically all of the new vehicles demonstrated that the LT influence was still prominent within the thinking of the new company. The Atlanteans and Fleetlines were delivered with traditional LT three-piece destination screens, and even the Reliances carried one-piece screens of similar dimensions to those of the elderly RFs. Internally, seat moquette was also to the latest LT style. However, some of the diverted Swifts were the first vehicles in the fleet to carry three-track number blinds and, despite receiving traditional Lincoln green, illustrated quite graphically that not all of LT's exacting standards were essential for what was now basically a provincial operator.

In the event, future vehicle policy was influenced very much by the National Bus Company, as opposed to any local initiatives. The new Leyland National, conceived by British Leyland with much influence from the National Bus Company, was intended to be the standard single-deck bus throughout the NBC's operating area. Although externally it was a very stylish vehicle, its interior specification left a great deal to be desired. London

Country eventually took delivery of 543 Nationals, the largest number ordered by any one company, and the type became London Country's standard single-deck bus. Subsequent orders for new double-deck vehicles saw further Atlanteans taken into the fleet, whilst for routes which were considered restrictive for larger vehicles a number of Bristol LHSs were acquired.

New vehicle deliveries remained fairly constant throughout the decade. However, despite this seeming abundance of riches, the company was about to embark upon a period when its credibility — both with its customers and with its own operating staff — would be stretched to the limit. It had always been accepted that London Country would be dependent for many years on the services of London Transport; the fleet contained many LT-designed vehicles, so the only real source of spare parts and maintenance back-up was London Transport. Unfortunately the unreliability of the newer buses inherited from LT, as well as some of London Country's own purchases, contrived to create the beginnings of a vehicle shortage from which the company would take many years to recover. So dire did the situation become that by October 1974 over a quarter of the fleet was delicensed, and many RF and RT types, covering for newer vehicles, would survive well past their intended withdrawal dates. In an attempt to reduce the impact of such shortages, buses were hired from other operators, starting in June 1974 with a large batch of AEC Merlins from LT. The following year saw the arrival of further hired vehicles, from Bournemouth Transport, Eastbourne Borough Council, Maidstone Borough Council, Southend Transport and Western National. While the Eastbourne contribution lasted only a few months, others, particularly those from Bournemouth and Western National, were far more enduring, the last hired buses not leaving the fleet until March 1978. During this time many new Leyland National vehicles were delivered, but conspicuous by their absence were further new double-deckers; other than three Atlanteans delivered in May 1974 and a small batch of Bristol VRTs in June/July 1977, none had arrived since 1972. This would change in March 1978, when more new Atlanteans commenced delivery. A further 170 had entered the fleet by May 1981 and these, along with 190 Leyland Nationals delivered in 1978/9, effectively swept the LT influence into the past.

Between 1975 and 1977 the level of OMO increased considerably. Many major trunk routes lost conductors as new Leyland Nationals eroded the quality of many a service. Some of these conversions should really have featured double-deck vehicles; replacing a 72-seat Routemaster with a 41-seat National was considered in many cases to be an act of sheer folly. However, no new double-deckers were available at the time, and many Routemaster vehicles were laid up awaiting spare parts; in order to return these to active service, some unfortunates were cannibalised and, in the majority of cases, never ran again. Indeed, this robbing of parts from defective vehicles affected many different vehicle classes, and ultimately a scandalously large number of vehicles never returned to service.

To ease the vehicle shortages, a number of different vehicle types were borrowed from various operators in the mid-1970s. Royal Blue Bristol MW coaches made their mark on local bus services from Dunton Green garage in October 1975 and were a familiar sight in the area for just over two years. Western National 1433 is seen at Pratts Bottom on route 402, a regular haunt for these coaches, in November 1975.
Phil Pickin collection

Plans were drawn up for the construction of a purpose-built overhaul facility, for which a site at Crawley was duly obtained. Unfortunately circumstances dictated that, by the time (1976) Central Works was open for business, a vast number of CoF-expired buses had been placed into store, and a huge backlog was thus awaiting attention. It was an impossible situation: the output of the works could not even keep pace with the rate of current CoF expiry, let alone deal with the backlog, and, although a number of vehicle overhauls were contracted to outside organisations, vehicle-availability problems continued to have an adverse effect on the company's operations.

By the mid-1970s traffic was being lost hand-over-fist as disgruntled passengers found alternative means of travel. County councils and London Country were continually in negotiation as means were explored to match service levels with available funding. The outcome of these negotiations saw economies implemented throughout the company's area as services were 'tailored to match demand'. Regrettably such measures also saw the closure of four garages — High Wycombe, Luton, Romford and Tring. Despite its best efforts, London Country still could not operate the revised (reduced) services with any degree of reliability, and an already fraught situation worsened. The company quickly gained a reputation for unreliability, and one which stuck for some considerable time. As is well known, a bad reputation is easy to gain but very difficult to lose!

The Green Line network also saw major changes throughout the decade. During 1972 new AEC Reliances replaced most of the Routemaster coaches, which in turn supplanted RTs throughout the company's operating area, bringing a touch of class to local services. The year also heralded the arrival of a batch of Alexander-bodied AEC Swifts originally destined for Western Welsh but purloined by London Country when the former company wished to divest itself of the order. Despite the arrival of these new vehicles, Green Line usage was declining quite dramatically. Indeed, OMO conversion of the remainder of the network was regarded as essential to stem mounting losses. Next it was the turn of the remaining RFs to see replacement, although in this case it was to be some of the company's first Leyland Nationals that would provide the means. Any hope that the traditions of yesteryear would be maintained was quickly dispelled by the arrival of these vehicles. 'Externally stylish, internally appalling' is perhaps the kindest description that could be applied to these buses. Endearing (!) features included inadequate legroom between hard, upright vinyl seats, a cold, stark interior and very high noise levels. Quite how much traffic these vehicles cost London Country is open to debate, but they

undoubtedly hastened the demise of a considerable chunk of the traditional Green Line network.

By 1976 the stark facts were that the vast majority of the long-established Green Line network was in terminal decline and that major surgery would have to be implemented if the name and any part of the network were to survive. Commendably London Country bit the bullet and took the initiative to restructure and promote the network. Many time-honoured route patterns were abandoned and all remaining cross-London services split, but the most visible commitment was the appearance of 30 new vehicles — AEC Reliances constructed to proper coach specification with Plaxton or Duple bodywork. At the time it was announced that 30 new vehicles a year would be leased over the next five years, but circumstances dictated that delivery should be speeded up, and all were in service by early 1980. Aided by an eye-catching new livery and extensive marketing, the revised Green Line operation became a resounding success and fully vindicated the company's decision to mount a rescue attempt.

The LT influence finally faded away during the early years of the 1980s. All traditional crew operation was gone, the few remaining conductors eking out their days on new Atlanteans. The last conductors were finally retired from Swanley in March 1981, and, given the economic implications, it is surprising that they lasted so long. All bar a handful of the redundant Routemasters were sold to LT, which returned most of the RCLs and RMLs to front-line service. The OMO vehicles — Merlins and Swifts — bought by LT in the late 1960s reached the end of the road with London Country in November 1980 and April 1981 respectively. Other acquisitions from LT had already passed away. The ill-fated RC-class Reliances were all withdrawn from stage service early in 1977, although a few lingered for some months as trainers. The mainstay of the inherited fleet — the RTs and RFs — last saw regular service in September 1978 and July 1979 respectively, whilst the very last ex-LT vehicle to survive — Fleetline XF3 — would finally expire in December 1981.

London Country Bus Services would survive as a company for four months short of 17 years. Its creation was brought about by politicians committed to the belief that a nationalised transport industry was essential for the wellbeing of the nation. Its demise — also a result of political dogma — was heralded as paving the way to the greater efficiency that the private sector could offer. Ironically, despite monumental problems in its formative years, by September 1986 (when London Country was split into four separate operating companies as a prelude to privatisation in 1987/8) its financial standing made it one of the best-performing subsidiaries of the National Bus Company.

A Personal View

MY knowledge of London Country's operations broadened considerably during my time in the company's employ at Reigate (1974 to 1978). My journey to/from Tolworth brought me into daily contact with London Country buses, and, despite the intervening gap of over 25 years, I can still clearly remember much of the day-to-day variety that I encountered. The 406 (Kingston–Epsom–Reigate–Redhill) was my usual method of getting to and from Reigate, and at the time the route was still predominantly RT-operated. Some RMCs had been introduced the previous year, but they were definitely in the minority and would remain so for some considerable time. Vehicle shortages meant that crew-operated RFs were a regular occurrence, mainly from Leatherhead and just once in a while from Reigate; these two garages shared the operation of the service. RF621 and RF655 were both regular performers for a while in 1975, although thankfully they seemed to be kept well away from LH55, the duty that provided my transport to work. This particular turn departed from Tolworth at 07.38hrs, which was an extremely well-loaded journey particularly south of Tadworth. At the time that I commenced my daily expedition to Reigate, it was, on schooldays, duplicated from Tattenham Corner into Redhill by RG19, which was scheduled to be an RCL but in reality could be almost anything! Above all, however, was the fact that RG19 was not a particularly reliable performer, especially when vehicle shortages began to bite, and many were the days when prospective clientele had the 'benefit' of a further 25 minutes to wait until the following vehicle arrived. Needless to say, in the fullness of time the duplicate was removed from the schedule altogether — an inevitable conclusion to the situation which developed thanks to the worsening vehicle position into which London Country descended. Unfortunately, as the state of affairs deteriorated, so the traffic was lost, in the majority of cases never to return, and circumstances such as this were commonplace throughout the company's operating territory.

During the ensuing two or three years I must have observed practically every operational variation that Reigate garage could muster. It became very much a case of 'anything goes', as far as vehicle allocations were concerned, and it is fair to say that, sooner or later, most types worked on most routes. However, for whatever reason, it appeared that RTs were kept away from the 405 (Croydon–Redhill–Gatwick–Crawley); should an RCL be unavailable an RMC would suffice. The crew route that saw most variety was undoubtedly the 414 (Croydon–Redhill–Reigate–Dorking–Horsham), as appearances by RTs, RMCs and any form of crew single-decker — RFs, MBs, RPs — were commonplace, if sometimes a little unpredictable. Scheduled highlights were the crew workings on route 424 (Reigate–Horley–East Grinstead) and the one evening crew working on route 430 (Redhill–Woodhatch–Reigate), both of which were officially RCL-operated but which could, again, produce any type Reigate had to offer.

I expended much film on the Reigate and Redhill scene during my time there and caught much of the variety on camera. However, if there was one working that could guarantee a problem, it was the afternoon crew RCL trip on route 430. This particular journey was covered by the infamous RG19, already commented upon above with regards to reliability. The afternoon scheduled workings for this bus comprised the 15.52 Reigate–Smallfield and 16.39 return journeys on route 424, which operated on schooldays only. On arrival back at Reigate (if memory serves me correctly) it then operated 'light' to Redhill to undertake the 17.42 departure to Reigate garage on route 430. The 424 workings were pretty reliable, but there always seemed to be a problem getting the bus to Redhill for the 430 journey. No doubt certain crews discovered that if they reported a fault with the vehicle on arrival back at Reigate from Smallfield then no other vehicle would be available for them and it meant an early finish. Not possessing my own form of transport at the time left me relying on such vagaries of public transport, with sometimes predictable results. The best spot to photograph this working was at Woodhatch, but its arrival was just a matter of minutes after the 18.00 727 had departed. This meant that I couldn't escape the area until 19.00hrs and, as happened on most occasions I went for it, it didn't run anyway! I lost count of the times I endeavoured to catch this bus on film — I twice managed to capture an RMC (once the London & Manchester Assurance overall advert, which was hardly typical), whilst on numerous other occasions crew single-deckers would appear. Generally, as the vehicle situation worsened so did the reliability of this trip, and sometimes it didn't run for weeks on end. The whole episode graphically illustrates the frustrations involved in following the fortunes of London Country, and one could easily relate to the hapless passenger standing at the side of the road who simply wanted to go from A to B! Unfortunately similar episodes to this were played out on a daily basis throughout the company's operating area and regrettably were not unusual occurrences.

In view of my associations with the Reigate area during this fascinating period of London Country's history, it seems as good a place as any to commence a tour of the network. Throughout the following I have deliberately not covered every route, schedule or vehicle alteration that occurred, although inevitably, as far as the demise of the London Transport influence is concerned, certain dates are recorded. What I hope I have conveyed are some of my personal recollections of the Country Bus network as I recall it, in the days before it descended to that of just another provincial operator.

Reigate

IN common with those at the majority of garages at the time of London Country's inception, operations from Reigate included a high proportion of crew work. Other than a one-bus allocation on route 411 (the main operation of which originated from Godstone garage), which gave rise to a solitary allocated RML, all crew work featured the ubiquitous RT type. Interestingly all crew work was based on shared allocations; not one service was wholly Reigate-operated. Reigate contributed to the operation of routes 405 and 405B (Reigate/Redhill–Manor Royal–Crawley), shared with Crawley garage, 406, shared with Leatherhead, and 414, shared with Dorking, as well as the RML on route 411 (Croydon–Godstone–Redhill–Reigate). Reigate also was the first garage to operate the 1967-built AEC Merlins, entry into service of which was delayed fleetwide due to a failure to reach agreement with the Transport & General Workers' Union over widescale implementation of one-person operation. Their introduction at Reigate was not considered a problem, however, as they simply replaced existing OMO RFs on route 447 (Redhill–Batts Hill–Reigate–Meadvale–Redhill–Merstham). Their entry into traffic was an acknowledgement that operating experience needed to be gained before their wholesale introduction, and they entered service in March 1968. Upon conclusion of trade-union negotiations, the following

November saw the introduction of the MBS variant of the Merlin to route 430 (Reigate–Woodhatch–Redhill). Whereas the Country MB variety was a standard 45-seat dual-door conventional OMO vehicle, the MBS variant was a purpose-built standee-type vehicle intended for busy routes with a high number of short-distance passengers. The MBSs introduced the concept of automatic fare collection to the Country Area and were branded as 'Autofare Buses'. The chosen method of fare collection relied heavily on the honesty of the clientèle; perhaps not surprisingly, the introduction of decimal currency was seen as a sufficiently good reason to dispense with the niceties of automation, and they were converted to conventional pay-as-you-enter vehicles in February 1971.

Reigate also possessed a sizeable RF allocation. Three RFs shared operation of the 447 group with the aforementioned MBs. Route 440 (Salfords–Redhill–Woldingham) was entirely RF-operated, and a one-bus allocation was made to route 439 (Redhill–Dorking–Newdigate circular), the main operation of which originated from Dorking garage. Green Line work on routes 711 (Reigate–London–High Wycombe) and 727 (Crawley–Gatwick–Kingston–Heathrow–Watford–St Albans–Luton) accounted for 11 RFs, while two of the unpopular RC coaches were used as spare vehicles. The 14 RCs — Willowbrook-bodied AEC Reliances — had been delivered in 1965 to evaluate potential replacements for the RF fleet. In the event it was decided to refurbish a number of RFs for continued Green Line work, and thus the plan for re-equipping the fleet was stillborn. Although undoubtedly impressive vehicles at the time, these coaches — basically standard AEC Reliances — soon gained a reputation for unreliability, and this was to haunt them throughout their careers, wherever they were used. Considering that other operators appeared to manage similar offerings quite successfully, one can but assume that unfamiliarity by the engineering staff was the root cause of the problem. In October 1970 an attempt was made to introduce the class to route 711, but they remained on that service only until the following August, when RFs returned. However, if Reigate thought it had seen the last of them it was very much mistaken, as they were transferred almost immediately to the 727, upon which they remained for a few months pending the arrival of new vehicles.

In the relatively short time it had existed, London Country had already made great play as to the average age of the inherited fleet and the fact that its long-term goal was to implement 100% OMO. Obviously this could not happen overnight, but an early announcement from the new administration was that of

Many crew services were operated by OMO vehicles on Sundays — a trend instigated during London Transport days and continued under the auspices of the new company. MB89 takes its stand time in the locally known 'Wood Street lay-by' at Kingston while undertaking such a duty on route 406. Kingston town centre has been extensively redeveloped since this view was recorded in March 1973, and, although this location is still just recognisable today, many years have passed since it played host to buses. *Steve Fennell*

new vehicle deliveries. Included within these initial acquisitions was a batch of 90 AEC Reliances intended for wholesale conversion of the remaining crew-operated Green Line routes. The Routemaster coaches displaced would transfer to bus work, allowing further withdrawals of RTs. Rather unexpectedly, the first of these new coaches to enter service did so in December 1971 on the 727, replacing the RCs, which were hurriedly despatched to Grays for Routemaster replacement. Grays was originally on the list to receive the newer vehicles, and one can imagine the reaction of the staff there when they discovered they were to receive these unloved six-year-old vehicles instead!

The eventual replacement of the RFs on route 711 fell to new 11.3m Leyland Nationals, classified LNC, in March 1973. Whilst perhaps suitable for relatively short bus routes, they were appalling vehicles for such a long-distance operation. These buses were among the first examples of a fleet that would eventually comprise 543 vehicles, making London Country the largest operator of the type worldwide. Only the initial batch of 70 vehicles was constructed to the 11.3m length, however, all subsequent orders being for the shorter 10.3m version, which was considered more manageable. Eventually a more refined 'Suburban Coach' style of National was obtained for Green Line work, and these later vehicles were much more suitable for the longer-distance journeys that such services provided. Unfortunately, however, the earlier bus-seated Nationals represented the nadir of Green Line operations and did little to help the case for long-term survival of the traditional Green Line network.

Five different classifications were adopted for London Country's Leyland National fleet, as follows:

LN	11.3m dual-door bus
LNB	11.3m single-door bus
LNC	11.3m single-door coach
SNB	10.3m single-door bus
SNC	10.3m single-door coach

There was no difference at all in the interior specifications of LNBs and LNCs, and initial deliveries of SNCs carried the

The RP coaches were part of London Country's first orders for new vehicles. Ninety were delivered, and the intention was to complete conversion of the remaining Green Line network to OMO. The overall advertisement bus was a 1970s phenomenon, and various examples afflicted most fleets as the decade progressed — some quite tasteful, others less so. Definitely falling into the latter category was the treatment afforded to RP46, which carried this somewhat garish scheme in an attempt to entice Joe Public to sample the gastronomic delights of Wimpy Bars! During London Transport days it was decreed that no external advertisements of any sort should deface Green Line vehicles, and the emergence of this apparition in February 1973 showed how attitudes had changed and standards declined. Quite a number of garages employed spare and mechanically suspect RPs on local bus operations; RP46 is seen at Redhill in July 1974 covering an MBS duty on route 430. *Steve Fennell*

same interior specification as SNBs. However, SNC116-202 were constructed to Suburban Coach specification, and their internal design was a considerable improvement on the standard bus product. Much confusion existed concerning Leyland National classifications over the ensuing years as 'coaches' were reclassified to buses. Ultimately all LNCs were reclassified as LNBs when removed from coach work, but the physical reclassification was not always undertaken on the vehicles concerned. Conversely some of the Suburban Coach variety received bus livery and SNB classification despite retaining coach interiors.

Between January 1972 and February 1973 a large proportion of Reigate's RT fleet was replaced by displaced Routemaster coaches. Technically there was no requirement for RTs after February 1973, but the reality of the situation caused a number to be retained for some considerable time. Indeed, Reigate's final RT was not withdrawn from stage-carriage service until February 1978 — some five years after the last had been replaced on paper. The first stage of the assault on the RT fleet occurred in January 1972, when route 414 received RCLs displaced from Romford. The infamous RG19 (see earlier) also gained an RCL from this date, thus bringing odd workings to

The conversion of route 406, shared by Leatherhead and Reigate garages, was a protracted affair spread over a number of years, as requirements elsewhere always seemed to take priority. Reigate's RMC1460 is seen leaving the town centre in March 1974. *Steve Fennell*

routes 406 and 424. Certain journeys on route 414 retained RTs; these were the buses that worked to/from Reigate to take up service on route 405 at Croydon. However, these workings lasted only until March, when further examples arrived for the operation of routes 405/B, plus an evening peak working on the 430. Originally it was planned that the 405/B would have received RMCs, the RCLs being destined for operation at Swanley garage. Physical restrictions at Swanley precluded this, however, and the vehicle types were exchanged, with the longer Routemasters gravitating to Reigate instead.

The 406 operation was next to receive Routemasters, and this time RMCs were the chosen form of replacement. A height restriction at Stoneleigh railway bridge precluded the operation of RCLs (and Atlanteans) on this service, as these vehicles' longer wheelbase and larger tyres caused concerns over the clearance available. In the fullness of time the bridge would be rebuilt to allow the passage of alternative buses, but by the time this work had been completed crew operation was very much a

thing of the past. The conversion of the 406 was a very half-hearted affair, and, although Reigate's allocation was technically complete, expiry of RMC Certificates of Fitness (CoFs) in subsequent months resulted in a 'temporary' return to RT operation. In March 1975 Reigate had a scheduled crew-bus requirement for 14 RCLs, five RMCs and one RML; serviceable vehicles allocated comprised 11 RCLs, four RMCs and one RML. Thankfully help was at hand, however, in the form of no fewer than five RTs. The RCL shortfall was normally made up by using the RMCs on RCL workings, the RTs being left to cover route 406. However, this was by no means the only option available, and RT operation on route 414 once again became a fairly predictable occurrence.

Reigate's one-bus allocation on the 411 (Croydon–Godstone–Redhill–Reigate) was nominally RML2308. When this was unavailable another RML was normally borrowed from Godstone garage, but as vehicle shortages worsened it became a regular occurrence to see one of Reigate's RTs or RCLs covering the working. The bus also worked some journeys on route 409 between Croydon and Godstone, although these were really only short workings of the 411, the LT practice whereby short-workings always took the lowest route number of any parallel services still being prevalent. For whatever reason, '411' was not included on Reigate's RCL blinds but 409 was (as, curiously, was 410), so, when an RCL did substitute, some compromise had to be made concerning destination blinds — usually involving a piece of chalk!

Reigate also operated some journeys on route 424. One of these was a morning-peak return from Reigate to Horley, worked by a 'coach before service' from route 711, whilst other journeys featured crew operation. Scheduled for RCLs, such work comprised a morning-peak and afternoon round trip between Reigate and Horley/Smallfield and a curious lunch-time short working between Reigate and Woodhatch which, on arrival at Woodhatch, partook of a 27min stand. This trip was very useful for Head Office staff making lunchtime visits to the Beehive public house, but seemingly served very little other useful purpose!

September 1973 saw the replacement of the Dorking–Redhill section of route 439 by an extension of route 425. MB conversion was planned from the same date, but the intended vehicles could not be released from Hatfield, and RF operation

London Country's sole Strachans-bodied Merlin, MBS15, became due for overhaul towards the end of 1972 and was sent to London Transport's Aldenham Works for that purpose. In the event, this work was not undertaken, and instead the vehicle was exchanged for a similar bus, MBS4, which had already received a pilot overhaul under LT auspices. MBS4 was thus repainted into standard NBC livery and re-entered service at Reigate, where it is seen on route 440 in April 1975. This unique vehicle later saw service at Crawley, Leatherhead and Windsor before being withdrawn in December 1978. *Steve Fennell*

Reigate garage had a one-bus allocation on routes 409/411, for which it was allocated a solitary RML. Whenever this was unavailable it was normal practice for a similar bus to be loaned from neighbouring Godstone, but shortages at Godstone frequently precluded this as an option. As a result, for most of 1974 Reigate regularly allocated one of its 'spare' RTs to the route; RT3450 is seen passing Godstone garage in April 1974. *Steve Fennell*

continued until September, when a partial allocation of Merlins was made. Further single-deck developments revolved around the eventual replacement of all MBs, MBSs and RFs by LNB/Cs, the first phase of which occurred in October 1974. Route 430 received LNCs displaced from Tring, and four of the redundant MBSs moved to Crawley. Four others remained, however, and were used to replace four of the five RFs on route 440. The following month, further LNCs arrived and partially converted the operations on the 447. Also replaced was Reigate's lone RF allocation on the 425, with an MB surplus from the 447 conversion. However, the 425 workings remained almost exclusively operated by an RF, thanks to the ongoing vehicle shortages. The official allocations from October showed a requirement for one MB for route 425, seven LNBs for route 430, four MBSs and one RF for route 440 and three LNBs plus one MB for route 447. This situation continued until August 1975, when service reductions enabled the last scheduled RF to be withdrawn. RF119 was despatched to Chelsham the same month, leaving RF134 as the solitary representative of its type at Reigate. However, only a few weeks later this sole survivor was transferred to Swanley (which was doubtless embroiled in yet another crisis over SM availability), and no RFs ever returned to operate in service from Reigate.

February 1976 saw the arrival of yet more LNCs, this time to effect conversion of route 440. All OMO bus work was now in the hands of LNBs (all LNCs transferred in having been reclassified, on paper if not in practice), other than the one-bus allocation on route 425, which retained an MB. The MB was also used on Sundays on route 406, as Leatherhead drivers had not been trained on Leyland Nationals. Despite the fact that all bar one Merlin had been replaced, Reigate was remarkably reluctant to part company with the species; three MBs and two MBSs, one of which was MBS4, survived into 1977, MBS4 moving to Crawley that February. The last example, MB110,

also moved to Crawley, in June, but the Sunday 406 problem had apparently been overlooked, as this bus was regularly loaned back to Reigate at weekends. Subsequently MB100 and MB109 arrived in July from Hemel Hempstead, and, although the former moved to Northfleet in August, MB109 remained until delicensed in November. Thus Merlin operation ceased at Reigate for the second time, but even this was not quite the end, as in April 1978 MB109 was resurrected and there arrived two MBSs rendered surplus by new Atlanteans at Crawley. MBS295/6 both subsequently moved to Garston, in July and May respectively, but MB109 remained until transferred to Dorking in January 1979. This definitely was the final curtain for the class, and these three buses represented the last members of the Merlin family to operate from Reigate. Despite there being no vehicles of the type allocated, Reigate's one-bus allocation on route 425 remained scheduled for an MB until September 1979, when the official allocation was adjusted to take into account the normal practice of allocating a Leyland National.

A programme of service reductions introduced in November 1975 saw the demise of the afternoon-peak RCL journey on route 430. The requirement for RCLs dropped by one as the morning-peak crew working on route 424 was replaced by an LNB, albeit surprisingly retaining crew operation. The lunchtime and afternoon RCL trips on route 424 survived at this time, however, as did the morning-peak RCL trip on the 406. However, the provision of a crew single-deck vehicle obviously failed to impress, as the morning trip reverted to Routemaster operation in January. At the same time, the 406 working was adjusted to commence from Tadworth in lieu of Tattenham Corner so that the same vehicle could be utilised. The 406 part of this working now operated considerably later than was originally conceived, with a scheduled departure from Tadworth booked at 08.34 instead of the previous 08.11hrs. Despite adjustments to the through service from Kingston, this journey now operated far too late to be of any use, and it was surprising that it survived until April 1977.

As mentioned earlier, Reigate relied very heavily on a number of RTs, all retained on an unscheduled basis. As at March 1975, five of these buses remained — RT3450, 4740/2/7/55. RT4747 moved on to Chelsham in June, RT4740 being delicensed the following month and subsequently withdrawn. The remaining trio survived into 1976, but January saw RT3450 move for continued service at Harlow whilst RT4755 moved out in February for further service at Chelsham. An arrival in April was RT981 from store at Grays, this bus being restored to service the following month. The other survivor, RT4742, moved to East Grinstead in June and was used on the special services associated with the Derby at Epsom Racecourse that same month. Thereafter it led a nomadic existence, moving between East Grinstead, Reigate or Godstone, wherever the need was greatest; its last garage was Godstone, from where it was withdrawn in October. Thus RT981 survived as the last of its type to operate from Reigate. Its CoF expired in March 1977, and this seemed to signify the end of RT operation from Reigate. Rumours of a limited RT recertification programme had been circulating for some time but were discounted as wishful thinking. However, during March it was confirmed that four buses would be recertified to cover short-term vehicle-availability problems at Chelsham, but quite unexpected was RT981's return to service at Reigate in May in traditional Lincoln green and canary yellow (as opposed to the standard NBC leaf green worn by the other three). On most days it could be found maintaining

earlier traditions on route 406, but by an unfortunate set of circumstances its final days came much sooner than expected. In February 1978, thanks to shortages within the training fleet, the bus was relegated to driver-training duties, and, although still carrying a valid CoF, never saw a return to stage-carriage service.

October 1977 saw the first assault on Reigate's remaining crew operation. Route 414 was converted to SNB operation, the vehicles for which had been licensed at Reigate from August and were thus already in evidence running as crew-operated vehicles. Withdrawn at the same time, without replacement, was the lunchtime crew-operated return trip to Woodhatch on route 424. To lessen the loss of crew work at Reigate, a further allocation of route 411 work was received from Godstone, and a couple of RMLs were transferred in as a result. Other changes implemented that same weekend saw the withdrawal of route 711 and its replacement between Reigate and Sutton with a limited-stop bus service numbered 422. The following month witnessed the arrival of further SNBs, which saw off remaining crew work on route 405/B. The 405B retained a limited amount of crew operation from Crawley garage, but Reigate's association with the route ceased. Also converted to OMO at the same time were the remaining crew journeys on route 424. Whilst a couple of Reigate's RCLs were moved to Chelsham, the vast majority transferred out to Godstone.

Saturday 28 October 1978 saw the end of crew work at Reigate, new SNBs and Atlanteans (ANs) providing the means. The SNBs, for route 406, were allocated well in advance of the conversion date, as the RMCs were needed at Chelsham, where CoF expiry was decimating the resident Routemaster fleet. The first example, RMC1478, moved in July, RMC1479 and RMC1504 following in August. September saw the removal of RMC1484 (albeit to Addlestone for storage following withdrawal), while RMC1477 and RMC1486 were both delicensed in October, having been the last of their type to operate from Reigate. During September three new Atlanteans arrived at Reigate for its share of the 411, similarly replacing the last three Routemasters — RML2308/13, 2446 — well in advance of conversion date. All three RMLs were moved to Addlestone for storage.

The use of RCs on route 727 was relatively short-lived, lasting only from August to December 1971. This was the second attempt to introduce the class on this service, but regrettably this was no more successful than the first! Unfortunately they had a notorious reputation for unreliability and seemed to be unwelcome wherever they went. New RPs replaced them *en masse* in December, whereafter they were transferred to Grays to permit the OMO conversion of route 723A. During the type's brief tenure on route 727, Reigate's RC3 waits time at Watford Junction station. *Colin Brown*

Godstone

AT the inception of London Country, Godstone garage was unique in being 100% crew-operated, with an allocation of 27 RMLs and three RCLs. The RCLs were employed on the remnants of route 709 (Godstone–Croydon–London, Baker Street) which operated Monday-Friday peak hours and also comprised two round trips on Sundays for hospital visiting. Surprisingly the service had the honour of being London Country's last scheduled crew-operated Green Line route, not succumbing to the pleasures of Leyland Nationals until May 1976. The route survived a further 3½ years until seen off by traffic congestion, the final journey, on 26 October 1979, being duplicated by prototype Routemaster coach RMC4.

A novel solution to vehicle availability problems was the acquisition in March 1975 of some Leyland PD3s from fellow NBC operator Southdown Motor Services. Three vehicles were obtained, rumoured to be the forerunners of a 'substantial fleet', although such plans failed to come to fruition. The trio entered service alongside RMLs at Godstone garage, where LS3, formerly Southdown 935, is seen on 20 September. *Colin Brown*

Bus operations at Godstone comprised RML routes 409 (Croydon–Godstone–East Grinstead–Forest Row), 410 (Bromley–Westerham–Oxted–Godstone–Redhill–Reigate) and 411 (Croydon–Godstone–Redhill–Reigate); also operated was the Sundays-only 482 (Caterham–Smallfield Hospital), but this service was an early casualty, being withdrawn in July 1972. All of these services were long-standing Routemaster operations, the garage having (in 1965) been the first in LT's Country Area to receive RMLs; initially insufficient green vehicles had been available and 17 red examples had been allocated for a short period — the only occasion where red RMLs operated in the Country Area.

The 410 received the first of LCBS's new OMO double-deck vehicles in February 1972, when 11 Northern Counties-bodied Daimler Fleetlines, diverted from fellow NBC subsidiary Western Welsh, replaced a like number of RMLs. In true Country-bus tradition, a couple of scheduled RML journeys remained on the 410 (and in later years a few unscheduled ones as well!), including a rather curious late-evening trip from Reigate to Westerham! The Fleetlines were delivered in a new, lighter style of green with a large broad yellow relief encompassing the waistband and lower-deck windows and looked

extremely smart; this livery styling was set to become the new standard for the incumbent and proposed OMO double-deck fleet. They also had traditional London Transport destination-blind layouts, which suggested that the LT way of thinking was still very much alive within the offices at Reigate. Some months later they increased their sphere of operation, appearing on the 411 on Sundays after the remaining Sunday operations at Godstone dispensed with the services of a conductor. Originally to be known as 'DFs', they were actually classified 'AF'.

The shortage of spare parts (and subsequently vehicles) that prevailed from 1974 onwards had a particularly bad effect on the company's Routemaster fleet. London Transport was itself desperate for Routemaster spares, and such parts as were available were directed to solving LT's own problems rather than those of an outside operator. London Country was very much at the back of the queue, and many vehicles (not only Routemasters), having been delicensed during the early 1970s, were simply cannibalised in an attempt to maintain others in an operable condition. March 1975 saw the arrival at Reigate garage of a Southdown Leyland PD3. As was the custom at Head Office in those days, a certain amount of paranoia was prevalent in case anyone found out what it was doing there, but soon rumours spread that a considerable number were to be acquired as a means to alleviate the prevailing Routemaster shortage. The 'considerable number' subsequently turned out to be three, and one can only speculate as to why it took almost four months to get the first one into service! Possibly the fact that they had manual transmissions had some bearing on the situation, but nevertheless, in view of the vehicle shortages at the time, it still seemed a little disproportionate. Classified 'LS' ('Leyland Southdown'), they entered service in July and August at Godstone, where they would survive a little over 12 months in service. Soon after their entry into service I managed a trip on one, after work one evening, from East Grinstead to Croydon. A nice little circular tour from Reigate, it involved an XF down to East Grinstead on the 424 and a short wait for the aforementioned 409 back up to Croydon. It seemed a little strange riding on such a vehicle in territory usually associated with Routemasters, and I got the impression that the driver was not particularly happy with his steed, although he had seemingly managed to master the art of changing gear quite successfully! On arrival at Godstone garage a vain attempt was made to swap the LS for an RML, and our (by now) none-too-happy driver resigned himself to the inevitable onward journey to Croydon.

Other than the OMO conversion of route 410 in February 1972, bus operations at Godstone had remained remarkably stable. Some variety had occurred in May 1977, when, to alleviate RML shortages, RMC1496 and RMC1501 arrived from Chelsham to assist on routes 409 and 411 for a couple of months, but the main event of 1977 was the conversion to OMO of the Forest Row journeys on route 409. This took place

The 482 was a legacy of days when specific services were tailored to hospital visiting hours. Over the years falling patronage virtually guaranteed the withdrawal of such routes, and at the time of London Country's inception only three remained. Of these the 482, latterly restricted to Sunday operation, was the first to cease, being withdrawn in July 1972. Photographed the previous month at Redhill, RML2320 was *en route* to Smallfield Hospital, apparently carrying nothing but a crew and a good deal of fresh air in June 1972. *Colin Stannard*

The 11 AF-class Daimler Fleetlines, diverted from the Western Welsh Omnibus Co, were London Country's first purpose-built OMO double-deckers. Once again, certain refinements such as LT-style destination screens and interior specification showed that (initially, at least) the LT way of thinking was still very much alive and well at the Reigate Head Office! These Fleetlines spent their entire working lives operating from Godstone garage, which AF7 is seen passing on route 410 in March 1974. *Steve Fennell*

in July, with a batch of 1972 Atlanteans transferred from Grays, although the conversion was not 100%, as some crew journeys still remained, notably those terminating at Lingfield, where a reversing movement precluded one-person operation. Also converted were the few remaining scheduled crew workings on the 410, but in the event the removal of crew buses from this service was to be extremely short-lived thanks to unforeseen vehicle problems. The 'acquired' Atlanteans were, to put it bluntly, not in the best of health. Godstone was already experiencing difficulties providing sufficient numbers of AFs for daily service, and inevitably it fell to the Routemaster fleet to provide the necessary support. Conversion of the 409 saw the transfer out of very few RMLs, as these (and the now spare conductors) were used to cover for the OMO vehicle shortage. Surprisingly most crew substitutions occurred on route 410 (as opposed to the 409, as might have been expected), and on most weekdays up to four RMLs could be seen on this long-established OMO service.

Vehicle availability problems carried on through into the winter months, and at one stage it was proposed to purchase a batch of Maidstone Borough Council Atlanteans which had been on hire at Chelsham since March. An example spent a few days on route 409 in October 1977 but failed to impress, and the plan was not carried through. As a stopgap, a number of brand-new SNBs were allocated in November, and these were used on all routes (both crew and OMO, as required) until their services were required elsewhere at the end of the month. Medium-term relief was available, however, from the end of November, when, following the OMO conversion of the 405, six spare RCLs arrived, and these stayed at Godstone until the following summer, when Certificate of Fitness (CoF) expiry began to take its toll. During their stay they saw service mainly on route 410, using spare conductors from Dunton Green.

In February 1978 RCL2219 suffered CoF expiry, whilst the following month RCL2259 was transferred to Chelsham for further service. However, reflecting the major problems still being experienced at Godstone, a further two examples, RCL2256/7, were transferred in during the first few days of April. By May, however, Chelsham's needs were perceived to be greater than Godstone's, and RCL2256/7 were both transferred across. RCL2229 had returned to Reigate some weeks earlier but suffered CoF expiry within days, and any use in service was minimal. CoF expiry claimed the last three

Two Lincoln-green RMLs wait on Godstone garage forecourt in October 1975. Both had been delivered new to Godstone in September 1965 and remained there for the whole of their Country lives. Both were withdrawn in September 1978 and sold back to London Transport in July 1979 to begin a new life in the metropolis, following overhaul at Aldenham Works. *Ernie Sargeson*

survivors, RCL2226/60 both being withdrawn in September (RCL2226 seemingly spending the majority of its final days undertaking driver-training work, despite having a valid CoF), and the final example, RCL2253, just lasting into October.

Further relief was at hand with the return of RMC1519 in May and also the arrival of two MBSs on loan from Crawley the following month. This was the first occasion that any Merlins had seen service at Godstone; they remained until September, when the delivery of new Atlanteans allowed their return. RMC1519 also moved on at this time for continued service at Chelsham.

Throughout this difficult period the majority of the service between Croydon, Godstone and Reigate had retained crew operation. Since July 1977 the remaining crew service had operated under the 411 route number, leaving the 409 for any journeys that penetrated south of Godstone (including the few scheduled RML workings to Lingfield). New Atlanteans were now in course of delivery, and it was announced that the remaining crew operation at Godstone would be converted to OMO from October 1978. The new buses were delivered in September and provided some much-needed relief, as by now CoF expiry was taking its toll on the surviving Routemaster fleet. The last two RCLs were withdrawn in October, although two RMLs (RML2330/44) were retained and continued to provide spare vehicle cover.

Such relief as was afforded by the arrival of the new Atlanteans was extremely short-lived. January 1979 saw the CoF expiry of the entire AF class other than AF7, which had received a pilot overhaul during 1978. Eight more were eventually overhauled and returned to service by the following September. However, in the interim all manner of different vehicles were begged, borrowed or stolen from around the fleet in an attempt to maintain services, perhaps the most unusual being an XF from East Grinstead. The two RMLs remained allocated and saw service most days, but RML2330 eventually suffered CoF expiry, in July, and RML2344 was transferred to Northfleet in August for a couple of months' further service.

East Grinstead

DOWN the road from Godstone is East Grinstead. Having paid a brief visit in LT days during 1969, when red MBs (MB379/80 from Crawley on routes 434/473), red XAs and a solitary red crew RF were in evidence, I did not return until July 1972. This was just a couple of weeks prior to the removal of the last remaining RTs at that garage — originally planned for that month but in the event deferred until November.

At East Grinstead, route 424 (Reigate–Horley–Crawley Down–East Grinstead) was home for five of the eight buses that comprised the XF class — London Country's small fleet of 1965 Fleetlines which originated as a result of London Transport's vehicle trials during the mid-1960s. As part of those same trials, LT purchased 50 Atlanteans (the XA class — 'X' in each case indicating experimental), and three of these also ended up with London Country, to be found at East Grinstead, in the main on route 424. The three XAs had joined the Country fleet in November 1969 in exchange for three RMLs. They initially entered service in LT red but were soon sent for repaint, reappearing in the traditional shade of Lincoln green. For the first six months of London Country ownership these buses were crew-operated, earlier experiments by LT to operate them as OMO vehicles off-peak, with the upper deck shut off, having

failed to inspire. This method of operation had been devised as a way around the lack of legislation to permit OMO double-deck vehicles, but it caused considerable scheduling problems and imbalances on both crew and OMO rotas at East Grinstead; indeed, it was cheaper to retain crew operation for the whole service, rather than go down the road of dual operation, no matter how attractive this might have appeared at first sight. Double-deck OMO was forthcoming, however, the necessary legislation having been passed in 1969, and the conductors on route 424 were subsequently dispensed with in June 1970.

East Grinstead's small RT fleet was employed mainly on the peak-hour routes 438A/C (Crawley–East Grinstead) as well as odd trips on the 428 (East Grinstead–Dormansland) and 435 (East Grinstead–Imberhorne Estate). They also operated 'shorts' on the 424 and 434 between East Grinstead and Horley and East Grinstead and Dormansland respectively. Once in a while one would be pressed into service covering an OMO working on the 424, running the whole length of the route through to Reigate, and I was lucky enough to stumble upon RT3125 doing just that on my visit that July. Another haunt was covering the one-bus allocation on route 409, when East Grinstead's sole RML was unavailable. The delay in replacement was simply down to the fact that the intended vehicles — the three XFs displaced from the Blue Arrow service in Stevenage in March — had still to be overhauled; in the event it was three new ANs that provided the means, but not until November. When the XFs finally did arrive it had already been decided that they would replace the three XAs, which (along with the remaining 47 examples still owned by London Transport) were destined for a new life in Hong Kong; the XAs were withdrawn in February 1973 and exported that April. The XFs stayed on, providing one of the few remaining links with LT influence. Interest was aroused by the liveries applied to the three transferred from Stevenage: two — XF6 and XF8 — were repainted in the new mid-green and canary yellow *à la* the new AN-class

East Grinstead's remaining RTs saw service mainly during peak hours, with random workings operating on most services. Some journeys on route 428 benefited from the presence of a conductor, and RT2499 is seen at East Grinstead performing such a duty in June 1971. *Peter Graves*

Atlanteans, delivery of which had just been completed; XF7, however, was the first of the class to receive the new National Bus Company standard livery of leaf green and white.

Following the RT cull of November 1972, ANs, XFs and (for a short period) XAs were all freely intermixed. Aside from the 424 and 438A/C operation, odd journeys existed on routes 428 and 435. One particularly interesting working in early London Country days which survived until September 1971 was that of a Godstone RML operating a morning peak return trip on route 428. Subsequent events saw the majority of Saturday operations on route 428 converted to double-deck, while, conversely, a couple of Saturday shorts between East Grinstead and Crawley Down on route 424 played host to RFs! However, there remained a very limited amount of crew work at EG, thanks to the aforementioned one-bus allocation on route 409. The nominal allocation, RML2306, was an early casualty of the spares shortage which in December 1973 rendered it unserviceable. (Indeed, it would never run again, being finally sold to London Transport some four years later along with the remainder of the Country Routemaster fleet and subsequently broken for spare parts.) In the interim Godstone assisted by loaning a replacement vehicle, right up until OMO conversion in July 1977.

On the single-deck front, East Grinstead maintained a number of RFs — not only for local bus work but also for operation on route 708 (East Grinstead–London–Hemel Hempstead). The bus operations comprised the balance of workings on routes 428 and 435 and a minority presence on routes 434/473 (Edenbridge [434]–Dormansland [434/473]–East Grinstead–Crawley Down [434]–Rowfant [473]–Crawley–Horsham), the main operation of which was undertaken by Crawley garage. First to go, in December 1973, were the coach examples on route 708, when new bus-seated SNCs arrived. These themselves were replaced in March 1975 by Suburban

Coach versions, and some of the displaced buses (reclassified SNB) remained to replace the small remaining RF bus allocation.

East Grinstead had been surprisingly free of the normally frequent bouts of service revisions inflicted upon other parts of the network, and, aside from a small scheme which saw the Edenbridge–East Grinstead section of routes 434/473 replaced by an extension of route 485 (Westerham–Edenbridge) in August 1975, the overall route pattern as far as local bus operations were concerned had been remarkably static. Perhaps inevitably, such stability was not to last, and 1979 saw the introduction of two schemes. The first, in January, saw the frequency of route 409 reduced to two-hourly south of Godstone and a re-routing to cover part of the 428 — itself revised to form a circular operation, still linking East Grinstead and Dormansland but also incorporating part of the 485 route as well as replacing completely the 435. Clockwise buses were numbered 428, whilst those travelling anti-clockwise carried the number 429. The October changes saw the withdrawal of the East Grinstead–London Green Line link and its replacement by a limited-stop bus service between Croydon and East Grinstead, numbered 409 and operated by SNCs. The 'stopping' service on route 409 was withdrawn between East Grinstead and Forest Row and the service substantially reduced south of Godstone. At the same time the 424 — long-time home of the XF class — fell to SNB operation, although a few double-deck workings remained. Overall double-deck requirements at East Grinstead fell to just five vehicles — three ANs and two XFs. A number of XF withdrawals had already occurred some months earlier, as CoFs had expired and only three serviceable examples — XF3, XF5 and XF7 — remained.

XF3 and XF5 survived into 1980, but what little remaining double-deck work that East Grinstead retained was converted wholly to AN operation in February. However, XF3 lasted until December 1981, ostensibly as a spare vehicle but still seeing

In London Country days the operating sphere of the XF class increased following their use as OMO vehicles. The short local service linking East Grinstead with the nearby Imberhorne Estate hardly justified the provision of a 72-seat vehicle, but interworking between this and other services provided the most economical means of operation. XF2 leaves East Grinstead with a scarcely taxing load one Saturday in April 1975. *Steve Fennell*

East Grinstead's last RTs were replaced by Atlanteans in November 1972. OMO conversion of the garage's remaining crew routes was deferred from July thanks to delays in overhauling XF6-8, which had recently been superseded by Swifts on Blue Arrow work at Stevenage. In the event the XFs were still not available, and the conversion went ahead using new Atlanteans. The XFs eventually returned at East Grinstead early in 1973 and were ultimately used to replace London Country's three XA-class Atlanteans, which were destined for a new life in Hong Kong. May 1972 finds East Grinstead's RT3450 waiting at Crawley bus station on the infrequent 438C variation; both 'A' and 'C' suffixes were subsequently dropped, all journeys then being numbered 438, officially from July 1973 but in practice some months earlier. *Steve Fennell*

regular use. The announcement made during the previous autumn that East Grinstead garage would close at the end of the year really came as no surprise. Since 1979 the area had suffered from seemingly endless service restructuring, in an attempt to reduce the amount of County Council support, and, with a final vehicle allocation of only 19, East Grinstead was clearly impractical to retain in the economic climate of the day. In the circumstances it was highly appropriate that the last workings undertaken by XF3 were on the 424, its traditional home since 1965. The curtain fell on 24 December when this bus worked a round trip to Reigate before being 'subbed' by an Atlantean, due to inoperative heaters. Significantly, XF3 was the very last vehicle of London Transport design to run in passenger service under the auspices of London Country. East Grinstead garage survived a few days longer than XF3, being closed after service on 31 December 1981.

Below: The XF class had a lifelong association with East Grinstead garage and despite sorties of varying lengths away from home they always eventually returned. Ordered by London Transport in 1965 alongside a batch of similar bodied Leyland Atlanteans, they represented a considerable change for those within LT used to more traditional vehicles. Only two XFs received the new mid-green and canary yellow livery before the NBC shade of leaf green was foisted onto unwilling companies; XF8 illustrates this pleasing variation in Reigate in June 1974. *Steve Fennell*

Crawley

THE Crawley area was an early target in London Country's quest to further the sphere of OMO. At the company's inception, such work at Crawley comprised a two-bus RF operation on route 426 (Crawley–Horley circular), whilst the 434/473 (Horsham–Crawley–East Grinstead–Dormansland–Edenbridge) had a seven-bus allocation made up of two RTs, three MBs and two RFs, of which the single-deckers were OMO. Additionally, two RFs were provided for a partial operation of local journeys on route 405B (Tilgate–Manor Royal–Redhill). Requirements for OMO buses did not match actual allocations, however. Only five RFs were allocated for a scheduled requirement of six, whilst, in addition to the three MBs, two MBS vehicles were also allocated, and these covered the RF shortfall. These were the first MBSs to operate in conventional 'pay as you enter' mode, the normal method of operation of these buses being through a pair of self-service ticket machines (marketed by LT as 'Autofare'). The crew-bus allocation consisted of no fewer than 28 RTs for a scheduled requirement of 24 plus three scheduled duplicates. Aside from

Despite the allocation of the majority of the SMA class to route 725, Crawley garage received one of the batch for local private-hire work. Needless to say, vehicle shortages soon necessitated its use on local bus routes; in March 1974 SMA20 is seen in the town centre on the relatively new service to Broadfield Estate.
Steve Fennell

the major proportion of route 405B alongside the aforementioned two RFs, crew operation consisted of allocations on route 405 (Crawley–Redhill–West Croydon) and town services 426A (Ifield Station–Pound Hill), 476 (Ifield–Langley Green–Crawley–Furnace Green circular) and 476A (Ifield–Langley Green–Manor Royal–Three Bridges–Pound Hill). Also featuring RT operation were the one-bus allocation on routes 438A/C (Crawley–East Grinstead) and the aforementioned workings on the 434/473.

August 1970 saw the RTs replaced on routes 426A, 476/A by a batch of new AEC Swifts. The order for these vehicles, initially placed by London Transport for the Country Area prior to the split, was passed on to the new company, and, although indications were that LT (had it retained any influence) would have used a proportion of them for RF replacement, London Country used almost the entire batch for straightforward crew/OMO conversions. Furthermore, this first batch of 48 were constructed with 38-seat bodies and came complete with a disproportionally large nearside luggage pen, where (allegedly) it was intended to fit Autofare ticket-machine equipment. One of the mysteries of the time, still questionable, was why the Country Bus & Coach Department insisted on its new contingent of Swifts (and for that matter the Merlins delivered in 1968) being built to dual-door layout when the Central Area managed quite satisfactorily with a proportion of single-door buses of similar manufacture. Typical of Country Area practice

Three RCLs were retained at Godstone garage for Green Line work long after all other such operations had been converted to OMO. Despite plans for their eventual replacement (which occurred in May 1976), RCL2237 caused a surprise by emerging from repaint in March 1975 with Green Line fleetnames on its leaf-green livery — the only London Country Routemaster to be so adorned. Its use on Green Line work was, however, minimal, and this unique vehicle spent most of its time on bus routes, as in this August 1975 view at Crawley. *Steve Fennell*

at the time was that these new vehicles, classified 'SM', operated some local journeys on the 405/405B and also strayed on occasion to the 434/473 operation. Conversely a limited amount of crew operation was retained on all three services, and this lasted late enough to see regular operation by Routemasters following the arrival of the first examples in 1972.

Southdown Motor Services operated a small number of local services within Crawley, and in April 1971 these were taken over by London Country and the small Southdown garage was closed; considered quite radical at the time, such rationalisation of work between adjacent operators eventually became quite commonplace as the decade progressed. Crawley thus inherited new services numbered 474/A (Gossops Green–Manor Royal), 475 (Handcross–Northgate) and 479/A (Bus Station–Gossops Green) — the former Southdown 76/A, 23A and 79/A respectively. The outstanding batch of new SMs were allocated for these services, but the 479/A, together with odd workings on the remainder (including one early-morning trip through to Handcross on route 475), received the benefits of RT crew operation.

Further erosion of the crew schedule occurred from September 1971, when three additional MBs and two RFs arrived, principally to allow the conversion of route 433 (Horsham–Lambs Farm Road) — itself a fairly short-lived operation, having been introduced only in June 1970. Converted concurrently was the majority of the remaining crew work on routes 434/473 and associated odd crew interworkings elsewhere. An element of service reduction also occurred at the same time, and, all in all, the arrival of these five OMO vehicles allowed the replacement of seven RTs. The same month saw the arrival of three Willowbrook-bodied Swifts dating from 1969 and acquired from South Wales Transport. London Country had had a reasonable degree of success in acquiring unwanted vehicles from fellow NBC operators, and these three Swifts represented part of a 36-vehicle contingent not required by the Welsh operator. A further 12 Marshall-bodied specimens in course of delivery to South Wales were also transferred to London Country. Unlike the three Willowbrook examples,

none of these 12 had seen service in Wales and were thus technically new vehicles; they subsequently entered service at St Albans. The remaining 21 carried Alexander W-type bodywork and were still under construction, so the opportunity was taken to amend the specification and incorporate LT-style seat moquette and destination screens — old habits certainly died hard! The Willowbrook- and Marshall-bodied examples were classified 'SMW' and, despite being attired in Lincoln green and canary yellow, looked very alien indeed. They were the first buses in the fleet to carry the provincial standard of three-track number blinds, which at the time was a considerable novelty for those used to London Transport's exacting standards of design. On arrival at Crawley the three Willowbrook examples replaced three standard SMs and were allocated mainly to those routes taken over the previous April from Southdown. They remained at Crawley throughout their working lives with the company and were finally retired in January 1981.

Crawley's last scheduled RTs were replaced in 1972. March saw the arrival of six RCLs displaced from Green Line work at Windsor; these comprised the main allocation on routes 405/B with inevitable interworkings which brought them to the 426A, 434, 476/A. Just four months later another three RCLs, together with three new Atlanteans, brought down the curtain on scheduled RT operation; the Atlanteans converted the crew journeys on the 474/A and 479/A as well as the one-bus Crawley allocation on the 438A/C, and the RCLs replaced the surviving RT workings, primarily on routes 405B and 476/A.

May 1972 saw the arrival at Crawley of one of 21 new dual-purpose Alexander-bodied Swifts. Classified 'SMA', these were the outstanding vehicles from the South Wales contingent, the majority having been used to convert route 725 (Windsor–Kingston–Croydon–Dartford–Gravesend) from RF operation earlier in the year; however, the vehicle allocated to Crawley, SMA20, was intended for private-hire work. The previous year a coach had been on loan from Southdown for this purpose, as a worthwhile amount of private-hire business had been inherited following the closure of the Southdown garage in the

Crawley and Northfleet garages held the rather dubious honour of being the last to operate members of the MBS fleet, the last examples being withdrawn within days of each other in November 1980. Officially the AEC Swift 691, the type was given the name 'Merlin' by London Transport, and this was subsequently used to differentiate between the MB and SM families, the latter being correctly referred to as 'Swifts'. Displaying the short-lived mid-green livery, MBS411 stands opposite Crawley bus station in May 1975.
Colin Brown

town the previous April. However, SMA20 saw regular use on local bus work when not used on private hires, and the introduction in November of a new one-vehicle service — 478 — between the town centre and the developing Broadfield area provided an ideal (albeit unofficial) home for it, in lieu of the scheduled SMW.

Further MBSs arrived in February 1973, having been displaced at Hatfield by new Leyland Nationals. They replaced some MBs and also the remaining scheduled RFs on routes 426, 434 and 473. Despite the best intentions to remove RFs from Crawley, during the next few years a fluctuating number remained in use as spare vehicles, and it was not until 1976 that the last two departed. Of these, RF567 moved on to Leatherhead in April whilst RF125, having spent some time delicensed, was resuscitated in June and moved on to Windsor; both had latterly spent most days covering duties on their traditional haunts on routes 426 and 434.

The arrival of the MBSs in February 1973 marked the beginning of a programme that, over the ensuing years, concentrated that particular type at Crawley; despite each individual vehicle running being designated an allocated specific type, from hereon the MB, MBS and SM allocations at Crawley were totally integrated in operation, with no regard for specific allocated types. The exception to this unofficial policy was the small batch of SMWs, which still held claim to the former Southdown services, although even that connection was broken in

September 1974 when route 426 gained an SMW allocation at the expense of the 478, which was converted to SM. More MBSs arrived in October 1974, displacing further MBs and SMs for transfer elsewhere, but by now availability problems, particularly with the LT-sourced single-deck fleet, meant that such vehicle transfers and subsequent vehicle allocations became somewhat hypothetical. Taking March 1975 as an example, Crawley had a scheduled requirement for 14 MBS and 11 SM types. At the time it had 24 Merlins and 10 Swifts allocated, so theoretically 34 buses were available for 25 workings. Included in this total were seven London Transport Merlins, part of a considerable batch which had been hired from June 1974 in an effort to alleviate the worsening vehicle situation throughout the company. Eight of the Merlins were delicensed, whilst only five of the Swifts were available for service. Thus only 21 buses were available for a peak-hour run-out of 25 (alleviated slightly by the allocation of a couple of RFs plus the private-hire SMA) — a situation sadly typical of most London Country garages at the time.

February 1975 saw the replacement of one of the morning-peak RCL journeys on route 434 with an Atlantean working, and thus the scene was set for the unofficial deployment to the route on Saturdays of two ANs, replacing two single-deck vehicles on the busy short-working journeys between Crawley Down and Horsham — undoubtedly an improvement for those clientèle who had regularly suffered a standee single-deck bus on a regular basis. This also relieved the pressure slightly on the hard-pressed single-deck fleet. Unfortunately such opportunity for providing increased capacity on busy services was not always taken, and in the fullness of time many crew services were converted to OMO using totally inadequate single-deck vehicles, such was the rush to dispense with crew operation. Eventually many of these services reverted to double-deck operation as and when new Atlanteans became available, but the scenario was reminiscent of the initial introduction of Leyland Nationals to Green Line work: the damage was done,

and how much regular traffic was lost, never to return, is impossible to quantify.

In February 1976 additional MBSs replaced SMs, leaving a mere four examples — SM122/47/8 and 466 — allocated against a booked requirement for five buses. A further swap occurred in May, following which, on paper at least, only two SMs remained, ostensibly the allocation for route 478. In practice, however, no SMs remained (other than SM122, stored unserviceable), as the surviving three serviceable examples were transferred to Dunton Green to assist with the replacement of the last RFs there. Service reductions in May contrived to remove three buses from Crawley's schedules, the peak requirement now dropping to 35. These reductions (of one RCL and two single-decks) put paid to the last few crew workings on route 426A. The SM situation remained static until October, no further Swifts being transferred in to make up the shortfall, as the vehicles simply did not exist in a serviceable condition. The solution, taking into account the reality of the situation, was to allocate MBS vehicles to the 478, and this was formalised in October.

Towards the end of the year the opportunity was taken to 'tidy up the edges' of Crawley's single-deck fleet. November saw the despatch of unserviceable SM122 to Leatherhead and of MB108, the last MB at the garage, to Guildford. MBS46, the last London Transport example to be retained by the company, was returned to LT at the beginning of December, and two standard MBSs were transferred in to provide replacement. Also to arrive in February 1977 was the unique Strachans-bodied example (MBS4), which settled down to regular employment on route 429 (Bus Station–Bewbush), introduced only the previous November to serve a further newly developed area of the town. Given the standardisation

London Country's long-term love affair with new single-deckers began to wane in 1978, when the first batch of new double-deckers to join the fleet for some time started to arrive in the form of Leyland Atlanteans with Park Royal bodywork. Many were destined for operation on Crawley town services, which were revised and renumbered with 'C' prefixes in July 1978. Prior to the revisions they were used to replace Merlins and Swifts on the existing network; here brand-new AN146 waits at Crawley bus station on route 429 in May 1978. *Steve Fennell*

on MBSs for single-deck work, a surprise was the return of MB108 in June. It lasted only a matter of weeks, however, until despatched to Dorking and was the last of its type to operate at Crawley. Also moving on in September was MBS4, transferred to Leatherhead. Crawley had lost its private-hire SMA in April, but two examples returned in November; ostensibly for use on contract work, in reality they made regular appearances on normal stage service.

November 1977 saw the OMO conversion of route 405 using the by now obligatory Leyland Nationals. This busy service should really have received double-deck vehicles, but none was available at the time, and, rather than defer the replacement of crew operation, the decision was made to press ahead using unsuitable 41-seat buses. The 405B journeys that operated north of Manor Royal were renumbered 455 and similarly converted. Three RCLs remained at Crawley for two scheduled workings, their work comprising a partial allocation on the remaining localised service on the 405B and, somewhat surprisingly, crew journeys on route 434. All other crew operation ceased, some of the displaced RCLs making their way to Godstone, where vehicle shortages were causing major problems.

By and large, the route network at Crawley had remained

Crawley's operation of the 434/473 service featured a *pot pourri* of different vehicle types, and this variety continued throughout the 1970s. The proportion of crew operation reduced over the years; during 1969 London Transport had commenced the conversion of the OMO part of the service from RF to MB operation, and this process continued under London Country, although the remaining RFs proved to be remarkably resilient, thanks to the general unreliability of the replacement Merlins and Swifts. Here RF122 covers for a below-par Merlin in March 1974 on route 473. Some journeys would remain scheduled for crew operation right up until the removal of the last crew schedules in July 1978. *Steve Fennell*

remarkably stable, in contrast to events which had occurred elsewhere in the company. Aside from the introduction of new services such as the 429 or 478 and the Southdown services inherited in 1971, the route pattern had remained very much as it was in London Transport days. It should therefore have come as no surprise when it was announced early in 1978 that the entire town service network was to be revised and operated by new farebox-equipped Leyland Atlanteans — a format subsequently adopted for a number of similar schemes introduced throughout the company's operating area. Following the results of a local competition, the revised network, introduced in July, used the brand name 'C Line', services being renumbered with a 'C' prefix.

Introduction of the C Line network put paid to the remaining crew work, although the last RCLs had departed three months earlier. New Atlanteans had started to arrive in April, and during the first fortnight an initial batch of eight had entered service, replacing some single-deckers and the remaining RCLs. These eight Atlanteans, used to convert routes 429 and 478 from MBS, also replaced the three 1972-built Atlanteans on the existing double-deck OMO workings on routes 434/438/ 474/A/479A

and were introduced — crew-operated — on remaining RCL workings on the 405B and 434. The remaining RCLs had all moved on by 12 April — primarily to Godstone, which was still experiencing chronic vehicle availability problems. Throughout May and June further Atlanteans replaced MBSs on a one-for-one basis on existing town services, and the proportion of double-deck operation on the 405B, 426A and 476/A thus increased. Following the restructuring introduced in July, just seven MBSs remained allocated, and these made up the main allocation on routes 434/473 and, from January 1979, a new 474 variation which operated via Colgate and Pease Pottage, replacing a service formerly operated by an independent. These MBSs proved to be remarkably resilient, and the last examples survived until November 1980 before finally being replaced by Leyland Nationals. Together with a small number retained at Northfleet, they represented the last of their type to operate for the company. It fell to MBS415 to bring down the curtain on MBS operation in the Crawley area, the last day being 14 November. The few remaining at Northfleet survived just a couple of days longer, thus robbing Crawley of the somewhat debatable honour of being the last garage to operate the type.

The local service at Horsham, between the town centre and the nearby Lambs Farm Estate, was a London Country initiative introduced in June 1970 as a crew-operated service. Such operation was extremely short-lived, however, and September 1971 saw the majority of journeys converted to OMO. In this undated view, no doubt taken shortly after OMO conversion, MB84 waits at Horsham's Carfax terminus before embarking on another journey to Lambs Farm. *Peter Relf*

Dorking

DORKING was another very small garage, with an allocation of only 28 vehicles at London Country's formation. It maintained a small fleet of RTs for its share of route 414, operated jointly with Reigate, but had a sizeable contingent of RFs, both for Green Line and bus work. Initially it possessed just one MB (MB82), for use on route 449 (Chart Downs–Dorking–Goodwyns Farm), but later in the decade further examples arrived, replacing a proportion of the RFs.

The 414 was an early recipient of displaced Routemaster coaches in January 1972, when the RTs were replaced by four RCLs from Romford, although, in the best London Country tradition, RTs were still to be seen on a random basis for some years thereafter. Indeed, at one stage in 1975, three of Dorking's four Routemasters were off the road awaiting spare parts, and both RT3252 and RT4495 spent varying periods helping out.

The RF operation encompassed routes 412 (Ranmore–Dorking–Holmbury St Mary), 425 (Dorking–Guildford) and 439 (Dorking–Newdigate–Dorking–Reigate–Redhill). The 425 was a shared allocation with Guildford garage, whilst Reigate had a one-bus contribution on the 439. Sunday operations on the 414 were also RF-operated. One of Dorking's RFs was out-stationed at Holmbury St Mary, and this would become the company's last regular instance of such a facility.

The removal of scheduled RF operation was a fairly rapid process, although, by way of a change, initial replacement was by AEC Merlins, six arriving in September 1973 from Hatfield. These provided a partial allocation on routes 425/439 as well as the Sunday allocation on the 414. Next to go were the Green

Line RFs, and this time Dorking did receive Leyland Nationals, allocated to routes 714 (Dorking–Kingston–London–Luton) and 712/713 (Dorking–Morden–London–St Albans–Dunstable/Whipsnade); these conversions occurred in March and April 1974 respectively. A few months later the RF allocation on the 412 was finished off by the arrival of two Bristol LHSs, classified 'BN'. The Holmbury outstation survived long enough for an LHS to feature, albeit briefly, as its use was terminated in November 1975.

All in all, London Country would take delivery of 67 Bristol LHSs. The first 23 were constructed to a width of 8ft and classified 'BL', while the remainder were built to a 7ft 6in width and coded 'BN'. Delivery of the former — BL1-23 — commenced in June 1973, while BN24-53 began to arrive in August 1974; a further 14 would be delivered in 1977 as BN54-67. All were originally intended for routes where physical restrictions precluded the use of larger vehicles, much in the same way that the GS class had been used by London Transport following the type's introduction in the early 1950s. Ultimately the BLs and BNs were superseded by larger vehicles as many routes were re-surveyed and found to be suitable for the more common SNB. Again, this was very much a case of history repeating itself, inasmuch as the fate of the GSs was sealed by the use of larger RFs on routes for which they were originally considered unsuitable (although the passing of legislation to allow the use of RFs in OMO mode was a contributory factor in that policy). Ultimately the LHSs were destined for relatively short lives with London Country. They

Upon formation, London Country retained on loan from LT five crew-format RFs to cover for general shortages of the type. The intention was to provide replacement vehicles 'in house' as soon as possible, but their stay in the erstwhile Country Area was quite long-lasting, with the final examples not returning to LT until February 1971. Throughout its London Country 'career' RF374 was based at Dorking garage, outside which it is seen on route 449. *Steve Fennell collection (photographer unknown)*

Many long-standing crew services were converted to Sunday OMO in LT days, bringing RFs to routes that would not normally be associated with such vehicles. In the fullness of time, most of these conversions received more modern vehicles, but unfortunately (or fortunately, depending on your point of view), as the decade progressed, RF operation could be guaranteed on all manner of services as maintenance problems forced considerable numbers of these newer vehicles to become static exhibits! One Sunday in March 1973 finds Dorking's RF304 at Reigate on route 414. RFs were then the scheduled Sunday type from Dorking garage.
Steve Fennell

did, however, provide welcome relief from the seemingly endless flow of Leyland Nationals, with which London Country seemed so obsessed, but, as seemed to be a recurring problem with new vehicles of the time, they were a very poor substitute for what had gone before.

A few RFs still remained, both on a scheduled and un-scheduled basis, such were the vagaries of London Country's allocation system. However, more Merlins put paid to regular RF operation from Dorking by March 1975, although RF175 managed to provide spare-vehicle cover as late as July 1977 before moving on for further service at Addlestone. Once Dorking's RFs had moved on, some of the magic of the place seemed to disappear. In the summer months it was a favourite area for 'pub-crawling', and the RFs were very much part and parcel of the scene; use of the rather spartan Bristol LHSs on the 412 seemed a particularly bitter pill to swallow, and this, coupled with the subsequent reduction of evening frequencies on many services, meant one's attentions (both bus- and alcohol-wise) were soon focused elsewhere.

October 1977 saw the conversion of the 414 to OMO with

Leyland Nationals. Dorking initially retained two of its RCLs — RCL2232/44. The former was withdrawn in December but RCL2244 was a little more enduring and survived until the following April. During this time it saw service mainly on route 449, with the occasional foray onto the 714. Next a start was made on replacing the remaining Merlins and, surprisingly, the two BNs, after only five years' service. Both events occurred in September 1979 when, somewhat unexpectedly, two RP-class Reliances were allocated to the 714, releasing Nationals to commence BN and MB replacement. Further Nationals were purloined, and by the year's end only two MBs remained on the books. During their final months these Merlins saw little use, however, and in the event lasted only until February 1980. They were the final members of the MB class to see service within the company, although some MBSs survived elsewhere for a few months longer. RPs were now being used in increasing numbers on bus work throughout the network, and it fell to that class to provide the means of replacement, Dorking having eventually inherited a total of five examples both for Green Line and local bus work.

Dorking's OMO route network was a long-standing RF operation which epitomised many parts of the Country Area network. RF replacement was inevitable, but hopes of any standardisation of types fell by the wayside with the arrival of Merlins, Bristol LHSs and Leyland Nationals. Dorking's last RF moved on in July 1977; some three years earlier, RF123 leaves Dorking bus station for Newdigate on the newly extended 439 route.
Steve Fennell

Route 414 was an RCL operation for over five years, having gained these vehicles in January 1972. They lasted until OMO conversion in October 1977, when highly unsuitable 41-seat Leyland Nationals would take over the service. March 1974 finds RCL2244 leaving the old bus station at West Croydon on this long and busy cross-country route on a short working to Capel.
Steve Fennell

The most visible sign that London Country was taking steps to alleviate its vehicle shortages was the hiring of buses from other operators. From June 1974 a number of London Transport Merlins were hired, and these subsequently became a familiar sight throughout the company's operating territory. The operation of red Merlins in the Country Area was nothing new, however,

MB379/80 having spent most of 1969 working from Crawley garage on routes 434/473. By the time the last such vehicles were returned to LT in December 1976, more than 40 different examples had seen service under London Country auspices; MBS70 is seen operating from Dorking garage on route 439 in June 1975.
Colin Brown

Leatherhead

ATLANTEANS could also be seen in Dorking, courtesy of the 470 (Dorking–Leatherhead–Epsom–Croydon), operated by Leatherhead garage. This was previously RT-operated, along with the 408 (Guildford–Leatherhead–Epsom–Croydon), both routes succumbing to London Country's new AN-class Leyland Atlanteans in June 1972. Prior to conversion both routes ventured across Croydon to terminate at Chelsham garage, with a running time of some 2hr 15min from Chelsham to Guildford and just under 2hr from Chelsham to Dorking. Such long OMO services were deemed to be impractical, particularly in terms of driver rostering, and it would also have brought joint crew/OMO running over the extremely busy Croydon–Chelsham section shared with the 403, which would have been unwise at the time from a timetabling point of view. Leatherhead had a considerable proportion of its services converted to OMO very early on in the LCBS era, route 418 (Kingston–Epsom–Leatherhead–Bookham) having the honour of being the very first service to be blessed with the LT-ordered AEC Swifts in June 1970. Information was not easy to obtain in those days, and the 418 conversion took me very much by surprise. I well remember being confronted by a brand-new SM at Kingston one afternoon shortly after the type's introduction, and, soon after, made a hastily planned expedition to Leatherhead garage to satisfy my initial curiosity.

February 1973 saw the arrival of two RMCs to commence conversion of route 406 from RT operation. However, one of the Routemasters shortly moved on, as needs were greater elsewhere. This left LH with one RMC, which turned out to be the only example allocated until November 1975. Even then, a period of this time was spent delicensed, and the 406 conversion, at Leatherhead at least, turned out to be a non-event!

As was to be expected, a number of odd crew-operated journeys on OMO services were scheduled. Coupled with this was the general unreliability of the Swifts, which virtually guaranteed daily appearances by RTs back on route 418. Rationalisation of the remaining crew journeys occurred in June 1974, when such gems as the afternoon short journeys on the 462 between Leatherhead and Fetcham and the 481 (Epsom–Wells Estate) ceased. Morning-peak and schoolday-afternoon 408 journeys still survived, however, and did so up until the end of crew working at LH in October 1978. Photography of these odd crew workings at LH was a frustrating affair, particularly when the possibility of RMC appearances entered the equation, and I personally had very little success in capturing RMCs on film, despite the odds' shortening as the number of RMCs allocated increased. LH53, occasionally my 406 home from Reigate, used to undertake a couple of round trips early evening on the 462. I was therefore in prime position to do something about it if an RMC appeared. RMCs on this particular running were as rare as hens' teeth, and the only occasion on which an example appeared prior to the withdrawal of the aforementioned 462 trips was a Reigate bus that didn't carry the relevant destination blind details. Needless to say, the week after the journeys were withdrawn, RMCs became extremely common on LH53! The afternoon 481 trip just occasionally produced an RMC; indeed, it did so on the afternoon of the 1974 Derby, when LH's only serviceable Routemaster, RMC1461, did the honours. Unfortunately my camera was being pointed at newly hired London Transport Merlins at the time. The 408 trips were just as exasperating: the morning working inevitably produced an RT but invariably showed '406' on the blind! On the two occasions that I made the effort, something went wrong! The afternoon workings were even worse, as the bus in question, LH60, undertook only a single Epsom–Guildford–Leatherhead journey with no other work; it was thus a prime candidate for cancellation due to vehicle shortages, and weeks passed when it simply didn't run. When Leatherhead's RMC availability improved, I felt inclined

Despite being the first route to 'benefit' from OMO conversion under London Country administration, route 418 still saw regular appearances by crew buses covering for Swifts. RT4496 waits time at Epsom Clock Tower one morning in May 1974 while covering LH41, then a regular working for crew substitution.
Steve Fennell

to have another attempt and, alas, failed dismally twice the same week — a Tuesday and Wednesday, I believe. A chance conversation with a Leatherhead crew on the Friday revealed that it had indeed run the day before — they had worked it! Naturally I wasn't impressed, and it was many years before I managed to pin down a Routemaster on the 408, in circumstances quite inconceivable in the 1970s!

Frustrations aside, the RMC:RT ratio gradually increased as more RMCs became available, and Leatherhead's last RT was withdrawn in March 1977, just over four years after RMC conversion began. Crew operation had not long to live by this time, and it was announced that the 406 and associate crew workings would be converted to OMO in October 1978. New SNBs were allocated from August onwards, operating initially with conductors, and the conversion took place as planned that October. Such was the situation with crew-bus shortages elsewhere within the fleet that, very much against normal practice for the time, no RMCs were retained at Leatherhead after this conversion; the majority moved to Chelsham for further service, whilst a handful were withdrawn due to CoF expiry.

The hired-vehicle revolution had come to Leatherhead in June 1974 with the arrival of some former London Transport Merlins, bringing red buses back into the erstwhile Country Area. Initially these covered RF workings on routes 468 (Effingham–Epsom–Chessington) and 481. Further arrivals in November 1975 saw the appearance of a small batch of Bournemouth Transport Fleetlines, which were used to relieve OMO double-deck shortages on the 408/470. Initially these Fleetlines had set running-numbers and operated Monday-Fridays only, but in the fullness of time their day-to-day allocation became considerably more fluid; notable was their use on route 418 covering Swift shortages. These buses represented just one of a number of options LCBS took up in the autumn of 1975 to provide sufficient vehicles for service, and they operated at Leatherhead until March 1978.

Much juggling of the single-deck fleet occurred between 1975 and the inevitable Leyland National invasion of August 1978, culminating in the gradual replacement of the garage's RFs. March 1975 saw the formal allocation of a number of BNs, resulting in the conversion of routes 416 (Box Hill–Leatherhead–Esher) and 419 (Langley Vale–Epsom Brettgrave). BNs also had booked work on routes 462 (Leatherhead–Addlestone–Staines), 468 (Chessington Zoo–Epsom–Effingham) and 472 (Leatherhead–Netherne Hospital). The last scheduled RFs were replaced in November 1975, thanks to vehicle savings made possible by the withdrawal of the 416 between Leatherhead and Esher and also service reductions on routes 468 and 481, although, as was normal practice at the time, such vehicles remained to provide spare cover. Circumstances dictated that RF operation at LH survived much longer and in fact experienced something of a renaissance in 1977, when three BNs were moved to Harlow to allow for the introduction of a new service requiring smaller buses. Three RFs — RF54, RF79 and RF218 — were moved in as a temporary measure in February, January and April respectively and spent the summer covering for the absent BNs. RF218 suffered CoF expiry in August, the other two following in October. However, the delivery of the next batch of BNs was accomplished in sufficient time so as not to cause any short-term problems, and Leatherhead received five of these new vehicles, two of which were intended to provide some relief from the ongoing shortage of SMs.

The short 481 route, which linked Epsom town centre with the nearby Wells Estate, was predominantly RF-operated, but some peak-hour workings were scheduled for a crew of two. The arrival at Leatherhead of new AN-class Atlanteans in June 1972 caused the majority of these odd crew workings to be replaced, but at least one afternoon round-trip survived until September 1974. In a scene reminiscent of one of London Transport's official photographs, RT4494 approaches The Wells in June 1972. *Gerald Mead*

Further variety was afforded by the arrival of a small handful of MB vehicles, initially on an unofficial basis, in March 1977. The type was certainly no stranger to Leatherhead, the garage having received a small number of hired London Transport examples from June 1974. Other, more interesting arrivals were a batch of former Barton Transport AEC Reliances with coach bodywork fitted with rather cramped 2+3 bus seating. These appeared on route 418 in October 1977, but their use on normal stage-carriage work was short-lived, and most were gradually transferred to school-contract work, for which their high capacity was ideal.

Concurrent with OMO conversion of the 406 in October 1978 was a major restructuring of the long-standing 418 route which also saw replacement of part of the 419 and the whole of the 481. New routes 476 (Kingston–Epsom–Langley Vale) and 478/479 (Kingston–Epsom–The Wells [479]–Leatherhead–Bookham) were introduced, and all featured SNB operation from day one. Initially insufficient of the new vehicles were available, and a handful of SMs were retained for a week or so until further deliveries occurred. Restricted (thanks to destination-blind constraints) to routes 419, 462 and 468, they were the last SMs used at Leatherhead. Most surprisingly, the replacement of Leatherhead's last ex-LT vehicles — RMCs, MBs and SMs — was an extremely rapid process, the garage thereafter operating a fleet of Atlanteans, Nationals and Bristol LHSs. All of Leatherhead's Merlins and Swifts were quickly despatched to the (by now) closed Romford garage, which was being used as store for withdrawn vehicles. The exception was SM503, which transferred to Amersham for a further spell of service.

Leatherhead garage was the first to operate the AEC Swifts originally ordered by London Transport, introducing them on route 418 in June 1970. Their sphere of operation increased over subsequent years, and later in life they became the prominent type on routes such as the 468. Repaint work was also undertaken at Leatherhead garage, and a regular sideline was repainting vehicles in and from Stevenage Superbus livery as scheduled requirements fluctuated. SM483 had been returned to Leatherhead for repainting in May 1976, a number of SMs having been replaced by further Leyland Nationals at Stevenage. Leatherhead, not wishing to miss the opportunity to alleviate its ongoing vehicle-availability problems, placed the new arrival in service; it is seen arriving at Chessington Zoo in June 1976, bringing a touch of colour to route 468. *Jim Macnamara*

A major OMO conversion which occurred in June 1972 was that of routes 408/470, which received new Leyland Atlanteans. Some eight weeks prior to the changeover, RT3120 approaches Sutton with still approximately an hour and a half to go before reaching Guildford. A handful of crew-operated journeys remained, however, and, surprisingly, some of these survived until the cessation of all crew work from Leatherhead, in October 1978. *Steve Fennell*

Further steps to combat vehicle shortages saw a variety of vehicles hired from many different operators. Bournemouth Transport supplied both Fleetlines and Roadliners, and, whilst the reliability of the Roadliners was a little suspect, the Fleetlines were considerably more successful, seeing service at Leatherhead garage from November 1975 until March 1978, generally on routes 408 and 470. Bournemouth 192 loads up at Epsom on route 470 in October 1977. *Steve Fennell*

Guildford

GUILDFORD garage was another that converted a sizeable proportion of its work to OMO early on in London Country days — so much so that by June 1972 no crew work remained, as new Swifts, Reliances and Atlanteans swept all that was familiar aside. Guildford was also a personal favourite; back in the 1960s it was my first real introduction to the world of Country buses and was the home, along with Addlestone garage, of the only lowbridge buses in the fleet, the RLHs. Unfortunately the RLH was destined for a short life with London Country, and all were replaced in one fell swoop in August 1970 following the introduction of a batch of new SMs. Guildford's RLHs were to be found mainly on routes 436/A (Guildford/Ripley–Woking–Staines) and 463 (Guildford–Woking–Walton), with odd trips on the 408A (Guildford–Merrow) and 415 (Guildford–Ripley). I managed a number of journeys on them in the weeks leading up to their

withdrawal and was quite sad to see them go. Some months later I 'discovered' the entire fleet gathering dust in Garston garage, the vast majority waiting their turn for export; their low height rendered them ideal for overseas use, and regrettably very few subsequently survived in this country.

July 1971 saw further Swifts partially convert routes 408A/ 415 to OMO, initially entering service some weeks before as crew buses to avoid the need to recertify RTs. Next to go were the Routemaster coaches on the 715/A (Guildford–London–Hertford) in April 1972, the final batch of RP class Reliances providing the means. Redundant RMCs moved to Grays and Swanley to effect RT replacement at those locations. The 715 had been the very first Green Line route to receive the then new RMCs in 1962 and now held the honour of being the last Green Line service to see them on a daily scheduled basis. The final nail was driven into the crew coffin only two months later, when new Atlanteans finished off the remaining RT operation on route 408 (shared with Leatherhead) as well as the usual selection of odd journeys elsewhere, primarily on routes 408A and Guildford–Burpham short workings on route 415, which sudsequently took the 436 number. The arrival of so many new vehicles in such a relatively short space of time was impressive, to say the least, but unfortunately appearance was not matched by reliability. To be fair, Guildford seemed to

A feature of operations at many places was the use of Green Line coaches on local bus work prior to operation on their intended routes. This practice represented a sensible use of resources, as a number of Green Line vehicles were not booked to depart from their respective garages until after 9.00am. RMC1465 leaves Guildford early one morning in June 1971 on a peak-hour trip to Ripley on route 415. *Ken Harris*

Following OMO conversion of Green Line routes, the new RP-class Reliances were similarly utilised on early-morning bus operations. In this March 1973 view, Guildford's RP88 has just arrived at Woking station, having covered a trip from Guildford; it will now return to Guildford as a 436 before embarking on a day's work on Green Line route 715. *Steve Fennell*

master the art of maintaining its new fleet far quicker than did some other locations, and the horror stories that were played out elsewhere as the decade progressed seemed to be noticeably lacking.

RF replacement was provided by MBs (route 425) and BNs (432) in September 1973 and November 1974 respectively, and from then until 1979 a period of stability reigned. As with all garages throughout the decade, a certain amount of 'mixing and matching' was apparent, in that vehicle allocation tended to be a little fluid. However, it was not until 1979 that the delivery of new Reliance coaches in April and Leyland Nationals in October allowed a vehicle-cascade programme to commence. The RPs displaced from the 715 by the new Reliances were subsequently cascaded onto bus work, enabling a start to be made on Swift and Merlin replacement. The small number of Merlins allocated saw relatively little use from that summer onwards, reliability being seriously lacking, and RPs and SMs provided cover as necessary. However, the arrival of the garage's

first Leyland Nationals allowed replacement of the remaining ex-LT buses to commence in earnest. Guildford garage was the last within the company to receive an allocation of Leyland Nationals, and by January 1980 sufficient RPs and SNBs were available for it finally to dispense with the services of the remaining Merlins and Swifts. All remaining Swifts and Merlins were withdrawn, other than SM110 and SM133, which survived as spare vehicles until the implementation of major service revisions in August.

Addlestone

OPERATIONS at Addlestone were always closely associated with those at Guildford. Many services had joint allocations, and work was regularly transferred between the two as resources were balanced throughout the years. Addlestone also shared the operation of the RLH class and, in common with Guildford, lost all its scheduled crew work by the summer of 1972. Whereas the operations at Guildford were relatively straightforward, those at Addlestone were far from clear, and, in the pre-1972 period especially, this was a particularly interesting area for the casual observer. Perhaps the best way to explain the situation is to reproduce the information in the form that it took in the company's official vehicle-allocation book, as shown in the table adjacent; readily apparent are the many different interworkings between buses and routes. Notable is the fact that Addlestone also operated on route 415, whilst Guildford worked buses on routes 461/A.

Such variety was inevitably destined for an early demise. August 1970 saw the replacement of 11 RLHs, one RT and one RMC by 13 SMs, and the opportunity was taken to 'tidy up' the remaining crew-bus work. Crew operation all but ceased, with what little survived being restricted mainly to peak-hour journeys.

An early casualty of London Country's quest for 100% OMO were the 17 surviving members of the RLH class, the only low-height double-deck vehicles in the fleet, based at Addlestone and Guildford garages. Inevitably they were replaced by single-deck vehicles, which materialised in August 1970 in the shape of LT-ordered AEC Swifts. RLH47 stands at Staines West station just a few weeks before withdrawal. *Peter Relf*

Further one-man operation was introduced with the conversion of routes 716/716A in March 1972. New RP coaches provided the replacements, but at one time serious consideration was being given to converting the routes to RF operation, due to physical restrictions at Richmond and Petersham. These were obviously overcome, but it would be interesting to learn which party originally voiced the objections — staff, police or local authorities. The displaced Routemasters all moved on to St Albans for bus work. Just three months later, in a programme virtually mirroring the demise of Guildford's crew work, further Swifts provided the means for replacement of the final RTs.

	Mon-Fri	Sat	Sun	notes
427/437/456/B	7 RF	5 RF	1 RF	also work journeys on 461/A/462
436/A/463	9 RLH	6 RLH	2 RLH	also work journeys on 415/461/462
420/461/A	4 RT	2 RT	1 RT	also work journeys on 415/436/437/462/463
	1 RMC	1 RMC	1 RMC	
	2 RLH			
462/B	2 RF	1 RF		also work journeys on 437
716/A	7 RMC	7 RMC	7 RMC	also work journeys on 420/461/A/463
Supplementary schedules	3 RT	1 RLH		
	1 RF			

The supplementary schedule buses cover works and school operations. RLHs must operate on all journeys on 436/461/A to Staines due to a low bridge in Staines Lane. Similarly all journeys on routes 436/463 that operate south of Woking have the same restriction due to a low bridge at Woking station. For completeness it should be mentioned that restrictions on double-deck vehicles also existed over parts of routes 427/437/456/B and 462.

415: Guildford–Ripley (daily) infrequent service
420: Woking–West Byfleet (Mon-Fri)
427: Woking–Addlestone (daily) extended to Weybridge Mon-Fri peak hours
436: Staines–Guildford (daily)
436A: Staines–Ripley (Mon-Fri)
437: Woking–Addlestone (Mon-Sat) extended to Weybridge Mon-Fri peak hours
456: Woking–Addlestone (Mon-Sat) extended to Weybridge Mon-Fri peak hours
456B: Weybridge–Byfleet–Addlestone (Mon-Fri peak hours)
461: Staines–Walton (Mon-Fri)
461A: Botleys Park–Walton (daily)
462: Leatherhead–Chertsey (Mon-Sat)
462B: Walton–Weybridge BAC Works (Mon-Fri peak hours)
463: Walton–Guildford (Mon-Sat)
716: Chertsey–London–Hitchin (daily)
716A: Woking–Stevenage (daily)
Note: 415, 436/A, 461/A, 463 operation shared with Guildford garage
462 operation shared with Leatherhead garage
716/A operation shared with Hatfield and Stevenage garages

The arrival at Addlestone garage in January 1978 of RCL2249 was extremely significant, as no crew-operated vehicles had seen service in the area since replacement of the garage's last RTs in June 1972. Generally operated during peak hours only, it settled down to a regular working on route 461 during the morning, the afternoon being spent covering various obscure workings on the 420/436/437 triangle in the Woking/Byfleet area, in the process managing to avoid the many low bridges that bedevilled the locality. Shortly after arrival it managed an appearance on route 716 and is seen here at Hampton Court on 19 January on what is believed to be the one and only time that such an operation occurred. *Geoff Rixon*

London Transport-ordered AEC Swifts provided the means of replacement for London Country's surviving low-height RLH class in August 1970; just a few weeks after the type's introduction, new SM142 is seen at Staines on route 436. On delivery the front panels of these Swifts were devoid of London Country's new 'Flying Polo' motif, giving the vehicles a somewhat austere appearance, although this insignia would soon be applied. *Colin Brown*

Keeping up the rapid momentum of change, February 1973 saw the arrival of more SMs. Displaced from Hatfield garage by new LNs and LNBs, these replaced the RF allocation on the 427/437/456/462 group of routes, thereby placing Addlestone's entire bus operation in the hands of the AEC Swift. On paper at least, it would seem, therefore, that Addlestone had gone from having the most interesting operational variations to the least. In reality, however, nothing could have been further from the truth, as the almost obligatory problems with Swift availability virtually guaranteed the sight of RPs covering bus duties, whilst a number of RFs remained allocated to provide sufficient spare cover. Addlestone appeared not to have a particularly happy relationship with its RPs either, and normally one or two could be found restricted to local bus work whilst their coach duties were either undertaken by RFs or cancelled. From a number of visits during this difficult time, I noted that the morning peak consistently produced the greatest variation.

Vehicle-availability problems as far as Swifts were concerned were commonplace throughout the company, and naturally Addlestone, having by far the largest requirement for Swifts at the time, suffered the largest number of problems. In March 1975, for example, the requirement was for 24 vehicles. Thirty SMs were allocated, of which 12 were, for various reasons, off the road. Six RFs made up the shortfall, giving 24 buses for 24 runnings, but clearly this did not allow for the effects of day-to-day mechanical ills. A major problem with the Swifts was the cooling system, and they were not particularly happy performers in hot weather, much to the chagrin of the engineering staff charged with responsibility for their operation. Conversely a winter problem was a distinct lack of working cab or saloon heaters, which didn't exactly endear them to the operating staff either.

When additional work was acquired in January 1978, most remarkably RCL2249 arrived and was used on a variety of local services before moving on to Chelsham in April. During its stay it also managed at least one appearance on route 716! This was the first crew bus to be allocated since the replacement of the RTs in 1972 and was also the only RCL ever to operate from Addlestone garage. Considering that the first stages of vehicle shortages made themselves felt in 1974, the fact that, some four years later, steps such as this were still being taken to maintain services serves to illustrate the seriousness of the situation.

Replacement of Swifts at Addlestone commenced in June 1979. The re-equipping of the Green Line fleet with new purpose-built Plaxton- or Duple-bodied Reliance coaches provided an additional source of vehicles for the company to use for this purpose, and the allocation of new vehicles to route 716 that month allowed the displaced RPs to make a start on replacing Addlestone's SMs. In October the garage took delivery of its first Leyland Nationals, and by the end of the year only four SMs were scheduled for service; altogether, seven SMs remained, the balance of three providing spare vehicle cover, and this allocation remained static until the following August, when a major service revision allowed four to be dispensed with. The three survivors, SM501/2/36, lasted until April 1981, thanks to a physical restriction between Chertsey and Shepperton on routes 459/461 which necessitated use of 10.3m vehicles. Eventually sufficient SNBs were procured to allow their replacement, and the last day of actual SM operation is recorded as 21 April. These three SMs were the last of their type to operate for London Country.

SMs were a familiar sight around the Addlestone and Guildford areas for many years; indeed, Addlestone was the last London Country garage to operate the class, the final survivors not being withdrawn until April 1981. Inevitably the traditional London Transport-inspired Lincoln-green livery gave way to the National Bus Company standard; SM477 in the new garb approaches Addlestone station in March 1978. *Steve Fennell*

Staines

PRIOR to October 1972 the allocation at Staines comprised solely RT and RF types, and it was not until some years later, by which time I was armed with a greater knowledge of the operational variety on offer, that my visits to the town increased.

The RT/RF monopoly was well and truly broken in 1972 with the arrival of MBSs, RMLs and RPs. First to arrive, in February, were a batch of RPs for route 718 (Windsor–Kingston–London–Epping–Harlow). The 718 operation was transferred in from Windsor at the same time, as it was found that the increased running-time needed for OMO conversion would preclude efficient scheduling if the service were to remain at Windsor. To balance work, Staines despatched some RFs, along with its share of route 725, to Windsor in a straight swap. The Merlins and Routemasters arrived in October, the former displacing RFs from route 460 (Staines–Datchet–Slough) and the latter (RMLs) eliminating scheduled RT operation, primarily on routes 441/C (Staines–High Wycombe/Englefield Green). Furthering the relationship with Windsor garage was the similar conversion from the same date of the latter's share of route 441. RFs remained at Staines for routes 466/469 (Staines–Knowle Hill/Virginia Water) and for Green Line work on the 701 (Ascot–London–Gravesend), 702 (London–Sunningdale) and 724 (Staines–Watford–Harlow–Romford). The inevitable interworkings brought crew buses to the 466/469 (although those on the former were extremely short-lived), whilst RFs were still booked to appear on the 460.

Further RPs arrived for Green Line work in February 1973, when the RFs were displaced from the 724. By now flexibility was the keyword as vehicle shortages contrived to make specific allocations difficult. In particular, it appeared that Staines did not get on very well with its RPs, and the inevitable RFs still made journeys to Romford (courtesy of route 724) on an almost daily basis. Conversely, the few remaining journeys on route 702 were quite often worked by an RP, as, operating at peak hours only, this was an ideal service for a bus that required maintenance during the middle of the day. The demise of the 702 was, perhaps, inevitable; shortages contrived to make the remaining journeys unreliable, and the route was withdrawn completely in July 1973. The remaining coach RFs retained for the 701 were themselves replaced by new Suburban Coach Leyland Nationals in September 1974, leaving just a handful of RFs for the 466/469 and associated 460.

Totally unexpected was the complete withdrawal of the 701 in October 1975, its SNCs moving over to route 724. This withdrawal was implemented at extremely short notice — less than a week — and at the time gave rise to accusations of unsound management. In fact the decision presaged the subsequent restructuring of the traditional Green Line network which commenced in January 1977, but it was a particularly bitter pill to swallow, and my own view at the time was that it could have been handled considerably better.

Staines also participated in the hired-vehicle share-out, when, in November 1975, a small batch of Bournemouth Transport Daimler Roadliners replaced the MBS fleet *en masse*. The Roadliners generally saw service on the 460 as well as the odd trip on the 466/469. They were notoriously unreliable and seemingly did little to aid the then current vehicle problems;

Leyland Nationals arrived at Staines in October 1976, replacing the last few scheduled RFs. At the same time, further Nationals presented the opportunity to dispense with the services of the hired Bournemouth Transport Roadliners, whose sojourn at Staines had not been an entirely happy one. The last RFs were mainly employed on the 466 and 469, RF67 being seen on the latter in July 1974. This particular bus would end its working life at Staines in April 1976.
Steve Fennell

October 1972 saw the arrival of RMLs at Staines garage, replacing all scheduled RT work, primarily on routes 441/C. The short local route 441C between Staines and Englefield Green seemed an unlikely choice for RML operation, but interworking and vehicle standardisation doubtless provided the reasoning behind such a move. OMO conversion, which might have seemed more logical, would not occur for a further five years at Staines, where RML2450 was photographed during September 1976 on the 441C.
Steve Fennell

by the time the hire was concluded, in October 1976, only one example remained serviceable. Following early experiences, it was fully intended that the hire period for these particular buses should be terminated after only a few months, but in the event they survived somewhat longer — presumably on the basis that an unreliable bus was better than no bus at all! Rumour has it that halfway through the contract period a rather one-sided letter was sent to Bournemouth from the Commercial Department at Reigate, listing the Roadliners' various short-comings, followed a few days later by another from the engineering department, requesting that the hire period be extended — a clear case, if ever there was one, of the left hand not knowing the actions of the right. The inevitable replacements were new Leyland Nationals, which displaced not only the Roadliners but also the few remaining RFs. As was traditional London Country practice by this time, a single RF survived at Staines. The vehicle in question, RF183, even received a repaint in traditional Lincoln green during 1977, although inevitably CoF expiry put paid to its forays on stage service, and it was withdrawn in February 1978. Throughout the last months of its operational career it spent the majority of its time working on route 718 (by now curtailed to operate between Windsor and Victoria) and represented the last regular (albeit unscheduled) RF working on the Green Line network.

September 1977 saw the OMO conversion of route 441. Again, Leyland Nationals were the choice for replacement, although, as with many other conversions during this period, double-deck vehicles would have been more suitable. Staines kept a few RMLs for some months after conversion, and, although most had moved on by the year's end, one was

retained until April 1979. For the last six weeks or so of scheduled crew work, Staines also played host to RMC1463, which (I believe) was the only occasion such a vehicle was allocated. Of the RMLs, two — RML2453/5 — moved to Hertford immediately following conversion, although RML2453 returned just a few weeks later. A further pair — RML2444/50 — moved out in November, nominally to St Albans as training vehicles, whilst RML2442/56 moved to Garston in December. It thus fell to RML2453 to provide a solitary crew-bus presence until April 1979, when shortages at Northfleet necessitated its transfer. It spent most of its time covering peak-hour journeys on route 441, but appearances on route 460 were not unknown. In February 1978 the 441 journeys that operated via Village Road in Old Windsor were renumbered 443. This was sur-prising considering that since London Transport days no variation of number had been considered necessary. Never-theless, Staines' surviving Routemaster had by now settled down to a regular running which involved a round trip to High Wycombe during each peak, the afternoon working now operating as a 443 in each direction.

Windsor

Windsor garage lost all but two of its RMCs in February 1972, when route 718 was converted to OMO using new RPs and reallocated to Staines; RMC1492/3 were retained to cover a morning-peak journey from Windsor to Datchet on route 445 before returning to Slough as a 460 and taking up 'late running' duties for routes 704 and 705 — if a coach were heavily delayed crossing Central London, a spare vehicle would be available to maintain an on-time departure for the return journey. RMC1493 is seen at Hyde Park Corner covering a trip to Victoria on route 704. More Green Line OMO conversions occurred from March, when the RCLs on routes 704 and 705 were replaced by further new RPs; the RMCs were thereafter confined to the aforementioned morning-peak journeys on bus work, and it thus came as no surprise when, at the end of April 1972, they were transferred to Swanley to aid conversion of route 477 from RT. *Colin Brown*

IN comparison with Staines, the operational variety at Windsor was considerable. My introduction to the area came in LT days and was the result of a family sightseeing trip. Inevitably the journey was by Green Line, and I distinctly recall having some success in persuading my mother that a homeward trip by RCL to Victoria and thence by train was infinitely preferable to an RF on route 725 direct to New Malden!

Windsor was one of the points where the 3xx-numbered routes of the Northern Area met up with the Southern's 4xx services. The former were represented by just two services, the 335 (Windsor–Watford) and 353 (Windsor–Berkhamsted), operated in the main by Garston and Amersham garages respectively. Nevertheless, Windsor garage had a minority share in both services, and in later London Country days these operations were among the more interesting variations of the area, with some journeys retaining crew operation long after OMO conversion at Garston and Amersham.

At London Country's inception, Windsor possessed an allocation of all three Country Area variations of Routemaster, as well as a sizeable number of RTs. OMO services were in the hands of either RFs or MBSs, the latter having been introduced on Slough town services in LT days to replace RMLs. A consequence of this and further vehicle exchanges instigated in the setting-up of the Country Area as a separate company was that all bar one RML had been transferred out. Thus RML2436 remained as the sole representative of its type until a further example — RML2418 — arrived in June 1970, the two then operating side-by-side with RTs on routes 407/A/417 (Cippenham–Slough/Windsor–Langley Village). Green Line services 704/705 (Windsor–London–Sevenoaks–Tunbridge Wells) and 718 (Windsor–London–Harlow) were operated with RCLs and RMCs respectively and, in line with company policy, were converted to OMO in February (718) or March (704/705)

At London Country's inception, operations at Windsor garage featured a high proportion of crew work. By 1980, however, this had dwindled to a mere one-bus allocation on route 407, for which two RMLs were retained. Crew-operated Atlanteans provided the means of replacement, the last recorded day of Routemaster operation from Windsor garage being Friday 13 February 1980. Just two days earlier, RML2422 is seen at Cippenham, carrying an unusual hybrid livery of Lincoln green and white with NBC insignia. *Mike Harris*

As the 1970s progressed, the Leyland National became very much part of the scene. When first introduced, some 30 years ago, such vehicles were very much despised by enthusiasts, much as new RFs and RTs had been during the 1950s; time mellows such opinions, however, and now the National has itself attained cult status, with increasing numbers entering preservation. One of the last routes to benefit from the type's arrival was the 458, upon which nearly-new SNB319 is seen in April 1978. *Colin Brown*

1972 respectively, using new RPs. At the time of OMO conversion the 718 was exchanged with Staines garage for the latter's share of route 725, as scheduling difficulties existed had the operation remained at Windsor. Although the coach rota now comprised a 100% OMO operation, two RMCs were retained for a short period to cover a journey from Windsor to Datchet on route 445, returning from Datchet to Slough as a 460. Such wasteful utilisation of resources was inevitably short-lived, and after only four weeks a revision to vehicle runnings saw an RT made available for these two trips, the RMCs moving on to more gainful employment at Swanley.

Further new coaches arrived during March 1972 in the form of the SMA class, allocated to route 725 (Windsor–Croydon–Gravesend). These vehicles were originally destined for South Wales Transport and were acquired by London Country when South Wales wished to divest itself of the order. They featured Alexander bodywork with a rather unusual rear destination-blind layout, but to all intents and purposes were standard AEC Swifts and thus had some mechanical similarity with other new deliveries. Visually they were quite appealing, but in hot weather they were absolutely appalling to travel on, adequate ventilation being an option that seemingly hadn't been included in the original specification. They were fitted with skylights which, when open, subjected passengers to a gale-force wind and, when closed, provided the effects of sitting in a greenhouse. In hot weather I avoided them like the plague, and they were a very poor relation indeed to the RPs which were in course of delivery at the same time.

As Windsor was bidding farewell to its Routemaster coaches, so further RMLs arrived to allow replacement of the remaining RTs. Indeed, by the end of 1972 all scheduled RT work would cease, although, as was almost standard practice by now, odd examples would remain allocated on an *ad hoc* basis to cover for Routemaster shortages. February had seen the balance of the 407/A/417 allocation and the 457/A (Windsor–Uxbridge) receive RMLs, the buses being released by an OMO conversion at Godstone. Further RMLs arrived in October from Harlow and Northfleet, allowing the conversion of the 441 from RT, Staines' allocation being similarly converted at the same time. Three RTs survived the Routemaster influx — primarily peak-

hour allocations, including the Windsor workings on route 353. However, such survivors were relatively short-lived, as three further RMLs were found the following month which (on paper) eradicated Windsor's last RTs.

Having been subjected to so many changes in a relatively short space of time, operations at Windsor saw considerable stability in the ensuing years. Operating economies inevitably occurred, but, overall, such revisions were more of a 'fine tuning' nature, rather than wholesale restructuring. One significant change which occurred in July 1973 was the renumbering of some routes, in some cases to avoid suffix letters. This brought about the sight of RMLs displaying 452 and 458 — the new numbers for the 457A/D and 417 respectively. Both services had previously been more readily associated with single-deck buses; indeed, the 458 still operated with RFs between Slough and Uxbridge, whilst the double-deck section was restricted to journeys between Windsor and Langley Village. Such renumberings were of questionable benefit, however, as it was to be some years before buses with three-track number blinds took over these services, and, in any case, not all suffix letters were eliminated. Initially Windsor's RMLs were reissued with destination blinds containing the revisions, and the whole exercise, whilst perhaps logical in the long term, at first seemed costly and unnecessary.

Further changes in June 1974 saw a reduction in the crew operation on routes 335 and 353. A casualty at that time was the one round trip, RML-operated between Windsor and Berkhamsted on route 353, which I personally classed as one of the top 10 London Country workings at the time; it ran Mon-Sat and produced a crew double-deck vehicle on roads which had long since lost conductors on a regular basis.

It would be the changes of January 1977 that ended the *status quo* which had characterised the Windsor and Slough operations for the previous few years. At the beginning of the month the remaining RFs allocated to route 458 were replaced by SMs, although the conversion was a very half-hearted affair due to vehicle shortages. Most of the RFs remained allocated, as at the end of the month a major OMO conversion occurred featuring routes 452 and 457. Also similarly treated were the RML workings on routes 335, 353, 458 and 484 (Windsor–

Slough town services had been converted from Routemaster operation to OMO in March 1969, using new MBS Merlins employing the Autofare method of fare collection. The reliability of the new vehicles was somewhat lacking, however, and crew buses continued to make regular if unpredictable appearances. Here RT4496 covers an MBS duty on route 400 in Slough in July 1970. *Peter Graves*

Standard fare on Slough town services for just on 10 years were the MBS class. Originally conceived as Autofare buses, following decimalisation in February 1971 they operated in conventional OMO mode before revisions to the town network saw them fitted with fareboxes. MBS413 is seen in the town on route 446A. *Steve Fennell*

Langley). At the same time, the through link provided by route 335 between Watford and Windsor was severed, although, following representations from Chiltern District Council, an RF-operated shuttle was introduced between Gerrards Cross and Little Chalfont. Not surprisingly, 'the shuttle' specialised in carrying fresh air and lasted a mere four weeks before its inevitable demise. This service was significant, however, as it represented the last scheduled RF operation within the company (although, as events transpired, Windsor's last RF, RF125, was retained on an unscheduled basis, not being withdrawn until January 1978).

The early-1977 OMO conversions featured SMs, as the aim at the time was to standardise on this type for Windsor's single-deck fleet. However, despite the best intentions, the vehicles were simply not available — a backlog of various CoF-expired examples awaiting overhaul being the reality — and the plan to replace the MBS allocation on Slough town services with further Swifts in July stayed just that, as the MBSs remained firmly entrenched. The OMO conversion of the 441 in October saw the arrival of the first Leyland Nationals, and, following on almost immediately, a start was made on SM replacement when further examples were used to displace Swifts from route 458. Single-deck bus allocation was extremely fluid around this time, with MBs, MBSs, SMs and SNBs all allocated. Ultimately (on paper, at any rate) the allocations stabilised to MBs on routes 335 and 484, MBSs on the revised 444/445/446 group (Slough town services), SMs on the 353 and part of the 452/457 and SNBs on the 441, the remaining share of 452/457 and the 458.

In February 1978 Windsor town services were revised and an MBS allocation was formally reintroduced, although the buses had never left in the first place. Also introduced in February 1978 was a new service, numbered 448, between Slough and Langley via the Trelawney Estate, which, although scheduled for OMO, saw frequent appearances by Routemasters — primarily RMC1513, which had arrived at Windsor in July 1977 and had managed to work the very last scheduled crew bus into Windsor on route 441 that October.

Backtracking slightly to October 1977, following OMO conversion of route 441 the scheduled crew-bus requirement dropped to one, for route 407. However, a number of surplus RMLs (and the aforementioned RMC) remained as cover for non-existent OMO types. This was now standard practice at most garages where conversions occurred, as there seemingly never appeared to be sufficient replacement vehicles to allow the conversions to go ahead; it also provided short-term employment for surplus conductors who were awaiting entry into the driver-

The highlight of Windsor's crew-bus workings was undoubtedly the round-trip performed on route 353 between Windsor and Berkhamsted. This operated Monday–Saturday and brought the sight of a crew bus to areas that had long since dispensed with this traditional form of operation on a regular basis; it also provided the twice-daily appearance of a double-deck bus at Chesham Broadway! In January 1974, some six months before the inevitable conversion of this working to OMO, RML2348 pulls away from Amersham garage forecourt *en route* back to Windsor. *Steve Fennell*

training school. In the event, six crew buses were retained at Windsor, and most days saw some unscheduled activity on routes 441, 452 or 457. By June 1978 the total had been reduced to four — RMC1513 and RML2348, 2411/5. The last was a September casualty whilst the RMC 'died' the following March, leaving just two RMLs to provide one bus and a spare for the 407 operation.

Replacement of the LT-sourced single-deck stock commenced in earnest from November 1978, when further Leyland Nationals were allocated. The intention was to replace all remaining MB, MBS and SM types, and indeed by the end of the year this had almost been achieved. The last two serviceable Swifts — SM500/15 — were delicensed in December (although SM500 was subsequently reinstated for service elsewhere), but two Merlins survived into 1979, MBS435 finally being withdrawn in March and MB97 succumbing the following month.

Changes to Green Line allocations were also occurring at the same time, as CoF expiry on RPs and SMAs contrived to cause further difficulties. Leyland Nationals were once again used to provide the necessary cover pending the delivery of further new purpose-built coaches, which started to arrive in March 1979. Windsor had already received a small batch of these in 1977 for the launch of a new non-stop London–Windsor route, introduced primarily to provide an 'up-market' service for the many visitors who would be making tracks to Windsor during HM The Queen's Silver Jubilee year.

The last vestige of LT influence thus fell to the two remaining Routemasters — RML2348 and 2411. On most days one of these vehicles would be found on routes 452/457 while the other maintained the scheduled crew operation on the 407/A. Also crew-worked were two positioning journeys on route 458 between Windsor and Langley Village. December 1979 saw RML2348 suffer CoF expiry, and surprisingly RML2422 was transferred in from Northfleet to provide cover. February 1980 saw their replacement with crew-operated Atlanteans; RML2411 suffered CoF expiry on the 11th, whilst RML2422's last day is believed to have been the 13th, the official date for conversion to AN being Saturday 16 February.

In contrast to other garages where crew operation was

retained after Routemaster replacement, that at Windsor lasted only a few months; service restructuring the following May saw the demise not only of the remaining conductors but also of the 407 itself.

Thanks to vehicle shortages, many garages either retained or acquired examples of RFs or RTs to assist in providing sufficient vehicles for service. Such stalwarts normally survived only until CoF expiry, but the help they provided throughout this difficult period should not be underestimated. In most cases, proper RT destination blinds were no longer available, and buses were 'dressed' as well as possible, normally using Routemaster items. RT1009, seen here representing Windsor's rogue allocation on route 441 in June 1975, carries masking on its blind glass and is fitted with Routemaster blinds but looks surprisingly tidy for what is really only a stopgap. *Steve Fennell*

High Wycombe

THE High Wycombe and Amersham operations shared considerable common ground. Should High Wycombe receive any service restructuring then it was inevitable that Amersham would also be affected, and *vice versa*. Despite such shared operations, Amersham had the rather dubious honour of being the first London Country garage to become 100% OMO, whilst High Wycombe retained crew work right up until its last day as an operational garage. The actual closure of High Wycombe in preference to Amersham was considered by many, both within and outside the company, to be ill-conceived. London Country still retained operation of many High Wycombe town services and now all buses and engineering back-up had to come from Amersham, some eight miles distant. Cynics argued that there now seemed to be more buses running out-of-service between those two points than carrying passengers. Coupled with the closure was the replacement of 72-seat crew buses by 38- or 41-seat Swifts on the same headways. Add to these problems the fact that the Swift was certainly not the most reliable of vehicles, whilst acknowledging that the whole area is notable for a number of quite steep hills, and the combination of fully loaded buses with high-revving small engines was a recipé for disaster! I well remember the occasions I departed High Wycombe on a well-loaded SM bound for Amersham on the 362; the climb up Amersham Hill was probably the steepest and longest in the entire London Country area, and it was rare, particularly in warmer weather, for a Swift to make it to the top unaccompanied by the sound of an 'Engine Overheating' buzzer!

On the whole, operations at High Wycombe were surprisingly stable. Other than changes of vehicle type and the inevitable renumbering of routes to eliminate suffix letters, the route pattern remained remarkably free from alteration, right up until closure. Crew operation survived on two services, the 326 (Micklefield–Mill End Road) and 363 (Penn–Totteridge), both using RMLs, although, whilst the 363 had received them in LT days, it wasn't until September 1971, under LCBS jurisdiction, that the garage's last RTs had been replaced on route 326. February 1971 saw the OMO conversion of the 362/A (High Wycombe–Amersham–Ley Hill), with new Swifts replacing RTs, although the High Wycombe share of these services required only two vehicles, the bulk of the allocation being maintained from Amersham. OMO work was covered by AEC Merlins, a batch of MBs having been allocated in LT days for routes 305/455 (Uxbridge–High Wycombe) and 305A (Uxbridge–Chalfont Common). RFs maintained the operation on routes 373 (High Wycombe–Penn–Beaconsfield) and 442 (High Wycombe–Hicks Farm Estate) and also on Green Line routes 711 (High Wycombe–London–Reigate) and 724 (High Wycombe–Watford–Harlow–Romford).

In October 1970 an attempt was made to introduce the RC class to route 711. These AEC Reliances had gained a reputation for unreliability which preceded them wherever they went! The fact that other operators appeared to manage similar

offerings quite successfully only serves to suggest that their unfamiliarity to the engineering staff may have been the root cause of the problem. Perhaps inevitably, their stay at High Wycombe was short, and RFs returned to the 711 in August the following year; the RCs moved on to cause mayhem on route 727, where once again their stay was brief! Vehicle-reliability problems aside, the popularity of the 727 operation, particularly the section of route between St Albans and Heathrow, was also giving cause for concern inasmuch as regular and costly duplication was required. Conversely the section of route 724 from Watford to High Wycombe was perceived, rightly or wrongly, to be poorly patronised. To solve the problem, from June 1972 the 724 was diverted from Rickmansworth to operate in parallel with route 727 as far as Heathrow Airport and then continue on to Staines, thus eliminating the duplication problems at a stroke. High Wycombe garage thus lost its association with this service, and an allocation was introduced in its place at Staines.

September 1972 saw the introduction of new RF-operated service 372, albeit only one journey in each peak between High Wycombe and Amersham, serving the Bruddenells School on Stanley Hill at Amersham. The RF proved hopelessly inadequate for the number of passengers travelling, and as a result the route was quickly upgraded to RML operation; this lasted only a couple of months, however, as from November an MBS was substituted. Further alterations that September saw the withdrawal of the 373 and the extension of Amersham garage's route 398 (Amersham Quill Hall–Beaconsfield) from Beaconsfield to Penn. One through journey during each peak was provided between High Wycombe and Beaconsfield, also numbered 398 but operated by High Wycombe, ostensibly with MBs.

June 1973 saw the arrival of LNCs for RF replacement on Green Line work, but, commencing in November 1974, the LNCs were themselves replaced by SNC Suburban Coach Nationals. Initially insufficient SNCs were available, however, and it was not until February 1976 that the conversion was completed.

Following the allocation of Nationals, High Wycombe retained just two RFs, intended for the one-bus allocation on route 442. This lasted until November 1975, when (most surprisingly, in view of the vehicle situation at the time) a 'paper' conversion providing an MB for this operation was actually carried through, RF196 being transferred to Garston. One RF did remain, however, such was the poor availability of more modern vehicles, but this last survivor at High Wycombe, RF673, suffered CoF expiry in January 1976.

The completion of the conversion of route 711 to SNC operation set off a chain of vehicle reallocations which affected operations at Crawley, Reigate, Hemel Hempstead and High Wycombe. Suffice to say the outcome as far as High Wycombe's workings were concerned was to replace the existing MB/MBS allocation with SMs. The MBs were

The LT Merlins hired during 1974 were spread far and wide. High Wycombe garage's MB123 has just arrived at Chalfont Common on route 305 in June 1974, shortly after the hire of such vehicles had begun. The Chalfont Common service originally took the 305A route number but was renumbered 305 in January 1974 to permit the introduction of new vehicles with three-track number blinds. *Steve Fennell*

Crew operation on High Wycombe town services lasted until the closure of the garage in September 1977. Thereafter the 326 and 363 both succumbed to single-deck operation using SM-type AEC Swifts — a type already prolific in the locality — and were transferred to the garage at Amersham. Just a few weeks prior to OMO conversion, RML2428 lays over at the Woodside Road terminus at Micklefield. *Colin Brown*

gradually despatched, mainly to Hemel Hempstead, whilst the solitary MBS gravitated to Crawley. The official MB-to-SM conversion date was set for February 1976, but, not surprisingly, the reality of the situation caused the MBs to linger, with the last vehicle, MB112, not moving on until May. However, in typical London Country fashion, MBs subsequently made a return, with MB83/6 arriving in October. Such vehicle transfers were typical of a period when allocations bore no resemblance to official records, and their arrival was an indication, if any were needed, that the vehicle problems which had befallen the company since 1974 had still to be resolved. The following month MB82 arrived from

Garston, but MB83 was soon despatched to Hemel Hempstead, whilst MB82 subsequently moved away in January. MB86 thus remained as the last of its type to see service in the area, surviving until closure of the garage in September. A point of interest concerning this vehicle is that it was one of the original batch of MBs delivered new to High Wycombe in 1968.

The last day of operation was Friday 30 September 1977, whereafter all local services were transferred to operate from Amersham garage. All crew operation ceased, and a route restructuring was undertaken which allowed for all town services to terminate at the town's bus station. Some renumbering of existing services occurred, with the 442 and 455 becoming the 365 and 325 respectively. Having operated to an emergency timetable (thanks to staff shortages) since August, the 711 was withdrawn throughout, the London–High Wycombe leg being replaced by a new 790. The choice of number reflected the fact that joint marketing was undertaken with City of Oxford Motor Services, whose High Wycombe–London express link was numbered 290.

RML2460 was the last Routemaster delivered to London Transport's Country Bus & Coach Department, in May 1966, and gained further fame quite late in its London Country career for being the sole example of its type allocated to Tring garage. Following overhaul in June 1973 the bus had a spell at High Wycombe garage and is seen that same month in High Wycombe town centre on route 363. *Steve Fennell*

Amersham

Standard bus RFs and NBC leaf green didn't really sit too well together, as demonstrated by RF640 at Chesham Broadway on route 336 in June 1975. Officially, Amersham's RFs on route 336 would be replaced by SMs between November 1975 and March 1976, but in reality a considerable number of the older vehicles remained to cover shortages of newer types. *Steve Fennell*

THE fact that the majority of Amersham garage's operations were predominantly rural in nature serves to illustrate how surprising it was, back in 1977, that it should survive over High Wycombe. Holder of the rather dubious honour of being the first London Country garage to achieve 100% OMO, it was also one of only two garages (Luton being the other) never to operate Routemasters.

Crew operation at Amersham finished on 15 February 1971, when SM-type Swifts replaced RTs on routes 353 (Windsor–Berkhamsted) and 362/A. Some of the Swifts had entered service prematurely from the start of the month to avoid the need to relicense RTs and had initially operated as crew vehicles, primarily on route 353. Amersham was also home to a small allocation of MBs, introduced in LT days to the 305/A operation shared with High Wycombe. The rural services were all RF-worked and at London Country's inception had accounted for a scheduled allocation of 13 RFs; just six years later, after considerable retrenchment, the rural network required a mere seven buses, by now all Bristol LHSs. Also RF-operated in 1970 was the 336 (Chesham–Rickmansworth–Watford) and a four-bus allocation on Green Line route 710 (Amersham–Uxbridge–London).

February 1971 also saw the withdrawal of the 710 between Uxbridge and Central London; the surviving stub was now no more then a limited-stop bus service, and perhaps the biggest surprise was that it lasted until September 1972 before being withdrawn completely, without replacement.

In February 1972 there occurred the first of many revisions to the rural network. Council subsidies to maintain loss-making services were still very much in their infancy, and this first round of revisions reflected the fact that Buckinghamshire County Council, although mindful of its obligations, did not feel compelled to foot the entire bill as submitted by London Country! Such were the intricacies of the area that any attempt to summarise the many changes that occurred over the ensuing years would be extremely tedious. Suffice it to say that this first round of changes saw the majority of links maintained, albeit in some cases requiring a change of bus at Chesham where a through facility had existed previously. The only stretch of road to lose its service entirely was the Great Missenden–Aylesbury section of route 359.

Following the 353/362 OMO conversions in February 1971, Amersham retained two MB vehicles for operation on route 305. Given its majority allocation of SMs, having two non-standard vehicles allocated was problematical, and in February 1973 these two MBs were despatched to Hatfield and replaced by two SMs. However, in April — just two months later — two MBs returned to Amersham in exchange for two SMs intended for Windsor garage's share of route 335. Windsor now possessed two non-standard Swifts amongst a majority fleet of Merlins, whilst conversely Amersham had a similar problem with two Merlins. Quite why such reallocations occurred is unclear, but common sense eventually prevailed, and the vehicles concerned were swapped back in July, after which no further Merlins were ever based at Amersham.

A fine view of RT600, still carrying obsolete Green Line livery from its LT days as a relief vehicle, at Chesham Broadway on route 362 in April 1970. The 362 epitomised the very essence of a Country Area RT route but alas was converted to OMO quite early on, in February 1971, using SMs. A joint operation from High Wycombe and Amersham garages, this conversion gave Amersham the dubious distinction of being the first London Country garage to become 100% OMO. *Peter Graves*

Unexpected was the allocation of Bristol LHSs in December 1973. Originally such vehicles were intended for operation at Northfleet, but physical restrictions on their intended routes necessitated a change of plan. Sufficient drivers had been trained to allow an allocation of three vehicles from December, with a further three entering service from January 1974. All the country services at Amersham featured scheduled appearances by these new arrivals. Concurrent with the January allocation was the renumbering of the 348A/B to 349 to facilitate their introduction, but, ironically, on the first day of the renumbered services the entire allocation on the 349 was operated by RFs. The basic rural network at this time was as follows:

332/398	Amersham Quill Hall–Penn
348	Chesham–Hyde Heath–Swan Bottom–Chartridge–Chesham
349	Chesham–Pond Park/Bellingham/St Leonards
359	Amersham Station–Great Missenden–Lee Common
394	Chartridge–Chesham–Tring

The level of service remained constant until November 1975, when further revisions removed another two buses from the schedules; the vehicle run-out now totalled 27 buses. Yet again, the rural network saw considerable reductions, the main casualty being the 348. Various restructurings took place, and it seemed that most villages surrounding Chesham were now served by the 349 or 394, such was the level of bifurcations introduced. At the same time the 336 received a partial SM allocation, and only two RFs remained on a scheduled basis. In reality, thanks to the poor availability of the resident SM fleet, seven RFs saw in the new year at Amersham and remained until their ranks were decimated by CoF expiry. March 1976 saw a 'paper' conversion which removed the aforementioned last two RFs, but RF55 and RF146 remained until July, when they were transferred to Garston due to CoF expiry of Garston's own examples used on the 309. As it turned out, this route was transferred to Amersham in January 1977, when it was converted to BL operation; reallocation was implemented to avoid the need to allocate LHSs to Garston, there being a perceived physical restriction on the route which precluded the use of larger vehicles.

The closure of High Wycombe garage from 30 September 1977 had a profound effect on the Amersham operations. Once again the rural network suffered from some pretty hefty service reductions, whilst part of the 353 allocation was transferred to Windsor. Despite this reduction in the original workload, as soon as the High Wycombe allocation had been transferred in, space was at a premium, and a number of vehicles were parked overnight and at weekends in the local 'Pay & Display' car-park! Additional SMs were purloined from around the fleet, the erstwhile High Wycombe crew work now being OMO, and for a few months Amersham was blessed with the largest SM fleet of any London Country garage.

A start was made on SM replacement in December, when eight Leyland Nationals displaced a like number of Swifts. The eventual replacement of the remaining SMs was a long-drawn-out process and was not completed until September 1979. Even after this date, four — SM145, 473/80 and 530 — remained as spare vehicles. All bar SM473 had moved on by the year's end, and this last survivor was relegated to the role of a training vehicle in March 1980.

To all intents and purposes the lack of any crew work at Amersham should have lessened my own interest in the area. However, Windsor's crew buses could still be seen covering trips on the 335/353 up until June 1974, and, of course, the poor availability of the Swift fleet prolonged the life of many an RF. It always seemed that RF substitutions occurred predominantly on the 362 in preference to other services, and the cynical view was that they could stand up better to the arduous nature of this particular route than could a Swift, examples of which appeared to maintain services on routes where the lie of the land was flat!

The 353 was converted to OMO at the same time as the 362/A, although the Windsor allocation, albeit only a minority share, did retain a number of crew-operated journeys for some years. SM453, by now in standard NBC attire (and with a destination blind that is distinctly lacking in route information), is seen at Windsor in June 1976. *Steve Fennell*

Nearly-new SM456 stands outside Amersham garage in April 1971. The arrival of these Swifts in February the same year put paid to the remaining crew operation at Amersham garage, giving Amersham the rather dubious honour of being the first London Country establishment to dispense entirely with the services of conductors. This was in line with NBC policy at the time and was to become a regular if somewhat depressing feature of route restructuring throughout the decade. *Colin Brown*

By the summer of 1976, with the last RFs gone, the area was devoid of interest from my point of view, but a subsequent event which occurred in 1980 led me to make what was by then a rare trip into Country Bus territory. The 2½ years of single-deck operation on High Wycombe town services had not been particularly successful. From late 1978 various areas of London Country's operation had been the subject of 'Market Analysis Project studies', and the outcome of one such study led to complete integration of both London Country and Alder Valley services in the High Wycombe/Amersham area in April 1980. Considerable restructuring of the local network was evident, but the highlight was the return of double-deck operation not only to Wycombe town services but also as a partial allocation on route 362, which was also extended from High Wycombe to

Marlow. Another new operation was that of route 345 (High Wycombe–Prestwood–Great Missenden–Amersham), worked jointly with Alder Valley but with the added attraction of some double-deck LCBS workings — it was many years since double-deck buses had been seen at Great Missenden! A number of 1972 Metro-Cammell-bodied Atlanteans were allocated, but, after only a short period of time, operating staff were expressing concerns about the hill-climbing abilities of said buses. The newer 1978-built Atlanteans had the benefit of an additional lower gear, and thus AN159 was loaned to Amersham to test its performance against the older vehicles. The outcome was hardly surprising, and that August and September a batch of new Atlanteans replaced the older vehicles, which were duly redeployed elsewhere.

Double-deck operation returned to Amersham in April 1980 following the results of a local Market Analysis Project. At the same time the opportunity was taken to integrate fully the local operations of London Country and Alder Valley and to provide a common route-numbering system. London Country thus inherited a handful of journeys on the hitherto wholly Alder Valley route 27 between Amersham and Great Missenden; AN111 is seen at Prestwood in June 1980. *Steve Fennell*

Tring

LIKE those at High Wycombe and Amersham, operations at Hemel Hempstead and Tring garages went very much hand-in-hand. Any changes in services and vehicle allocation at Hemel Hempstead invariably had some effect at Tring. Some would say that Tring was almost a sub-shed of Hemel Hempstead, but no doubt the staff that were based at this small but friendly garage would have had a different opinion!

Tring's allocation comprised crew work on route 301 (Aylesbury–Little Bushey), with an allocation of the ubiquitous RT type, and Green Line work on route 706 (Aylesbury–London–Chelsham), with the inevitable RFs. Also at Tring was the unique Strachans-bodied AEC Merlin (MBS15) allocated to route 387 (Tring–Aldbury), which represented the survivor in the Country fleet of an experimental batch of nine vehicles delivered during 1966. These nine buses were originally intended to operate as conventional 46-seat OMO vehicles from Addlestone garage, replacing RFs on local services. However, no agreement for their use could be reached with the Trade Union. Subsequent events dictated that the majority would see service in the Central Area, where the success of the recently introduced Red Arrow service meant that additional resources were required, and all bar one were thus transferred to Central Area stock. The sole survivor was used for a number of different purposes before settling at Tring and making its home on the 387. During the winter of 1972/3 the vehicle became due for overhaul and was transferred to London Transport's Aldenham Works for this purpose, but the work was never started and instead it was exchanged with another Strachans-

bodied example which had recently been so treated. However, Tring would not see this bus, as, upon delivery to London Country, it was allocated to Reigate. During February 1973 Tring thus received (from Hemel Hempstead) MBS295, a standard MBS, which remained until the arrival of Leyland Nationals brought about its replacement.

Tring was the second garage within the London Country empire to benefit from the arrival of Leyland Nationals for Green Line work when a batch of 11.3m buses arrived to replace the RFs on route 706 from March 1973. As was typical at the time, these vehicles were the standard bus product, with no refinements for their intended role as medium-to-long-distance transport. In the fullness of time they were eventually replaced by 10.3m Suburban Coach examples, the first of which arrived in October 1974, but, as with so many Green Line services at the time that were plagued with these vehicles, the long-term damage had been done.

Further Nationals arrived in May 1975, when route 301 was converted to OMO, replacing, in one fell swoop, the garage's entire RT fleet. Remaining crew work included a small allocation on route 312 (Hemel Hempstead–Berkhamsted), which had some journeys extended to Tring for this purpose. Two crew buses were required for this operation, and these materialised in the form of a pair of RMCs — the first allocation of Routemasters to this garage. Some crew journeys were also retained on route 387 to/from Tring station (the section thence to Aldbury being restricted to single-deck operation due to overhanging trees), and these were covered by

By 1977 the combination of ever-increasing operating costs and service reductions had created considerable spare capacity within the company, and inevitably thoughts turned to garage closures. The year saw four garages — Luton, Tring, Romford and High Wycombe — pass into history. Each was a victim of economics, but for operating staff, a number of whom had worked at these garages for many years, it was a very sad time. Tring garage's swansong was undoubtedly the regular operation of an RT on route 706, which lasted from June 1976 until February 1977, initially using RT3530 and, from September, RT3631. Regrettably I managed only one such RT trip during this time, on an evening-peak working from London to Aylesbury in January 1977. Suffice it to say a 20min loss of time between Victoria and Edgware was followed by a 5min-early arrival at Aylesbury. RT3631 stands at Aylesbury bus station after its exhilarating run from Central London. *Steve Fennell*

Prior to May 1975 a number of am and pm journeys on route 387 were crew-operated, using RTs. Following OMO conversion of the 301 and the removal of Tring's RT fleet, only a handful of morning workings remained thus, being operated either by RMCs or (latterly) RML2460. RMC1513 is shown at Tring station on one such working in June 1976. *Steve Fennell*

the same two RMCs. On impulse, on the last day of crew operation on route 301 I decided to travel on the very last RT journey. This came about by a number of factors: firstly, due to staff shortages, the actual service operated from Tring (and, for that matter, Hemel Hempstead) that evening bore no resemblance to that planned, and therefore the last RT was due to run in just after 22.00hrs; the essential ingredient, however, was the offer of a lift to Cricklewood, from where I could take a night bus into Central London, in the hope of finding a train home. Fortune certainly smiled on the foolish that night, as, on arrival at Waterloo station, I discovered I had only a matter of minutes to spare before my last train home for some considerable time! Back at Tring, RT4751 had performed the honours, and I clearly recall an extremely high-speed journey from Watford through to Aylesbury and then back to Tring. The final trip that evening was looked upon very much as the end of an era, but unbeknown at the time to all present, an RT would again see service from Tring. As was so usual during this fascinating period, the circumstances of the subsequent return would have been looked upon with disbelief and considered pure fantasy, had they even been suggested at the time!

In August 1975 one of the workings on the 312 was nominally converted to RML, but this was yet another of the 'paper' conversions of which London Country seemed so fond at the time, and no changes to actual vehicle allocation occurred. November saw the remaining RMC duty similarly converted, except that this time an RML actually made its way to Tring. However, despite the allocation being officially 2 x RML, no further examples of this type were ever transferred, and the actual crew operation remained as one RMC and one RML.

In terms of crew work, the best was yet to come, as in June 1976 RT3530 arrived from Garston and was immediately put

to work on Green Line route 706. The RT settled down to a regular routine, performing peak-hour work between Aylesbury and Victoria — one round trip in each peak. On occasion, however, it found its way right through to Chelsham and on one Saturday was loaned to Hemel Hempstead to operate on route 708, albeit only to/from London. At the time such operation was considered only a short-term option, but amazingly it continued: when RT3530 returned to Garston in September this was thought to be the end, but, incredibly, RT3631 arrived a few days later from Luton and maintained the same operation until CoF expiry claimed it during February 1977. During this time a full front set of proper Green Line RT destination blinds was produced by a friend of mine, Peter Graves, and this was really the icing on the cake. Regular predictable five-days-a-week RT operation on Green Line work had not been seen since the mid-1960s, and these workings were very much a highlight at the time.

Unfortunately the RT renaissance proved to be Tring garage's swansong; rumours had been circulating for some time concerning closure, and it was duly announced at the end of 1976 that this would occur by April of the following year. The last day of operation from Tring was Friday 31 March 1977. The Aylesbury leg of the 706 was covered by an extension of the 708 from Hemel Hempstead, the 312 and remaining crew work were replaced by alterations to the main 301 service, and all surviving bus work, including the workings on route 387, was transferred to Hemel Hempstead.

Tring's demise was inevitable as county councils attempted to keep subsidies for public transport under control, but, as was so often the case, such decisions were taken around a table by people who had little regard for tradition or the effect that their policy would have on an ever more beleaguered workforce.

Hemel Hempstead

COMPARED with those at Tring, operations at Hemel Hempstead (Two Waters) garage were extremely intricate. Interworkings were rife, and the town area possessed a convoluted web of routes designed to serve the vast industrial estates at Maylands Avenue and Apsley Mills. Many services operated only a handful of journeys each day and (more often than not) featured differing vehicle types. As always, the variations in day-to-day operation were increased by vehicle shortages, although, as the decade progressed and the ubiquitous Leyland National made its presence felt, the operational variety diminished.

One of the joys of photography at Hemel Hempstead was the lunchtime procession to Apsley Mills. However, the major problem here was the reluctance or inability of some of the crews to display correct destination details — a somewhat frustrating feature, considering the paucity of many of these works services. The solution was therefore to do it yourself! Many were the times I walked into the garage at Two Waters to view the vehicle-allocation sheet, found the lunchtime run-out had not yet been plated up and was handed a selection of running-number plates and duty boards and told to 'sort it out if you like'. I would then spend 30 minutes or so ensuring that all buses were correctly 'dressed' before making my way to the Mills turning-circle to await the fun. An added bonus was that I got two performances per lunch hour, as the buses all made a round trip to and from the Mills.

Hemel's crew allocation initially comprised a vast number of RTs, as well as two RMLs for its small portion of route 347/A (Hemel Hempstead–Watford–Uxbridge), shared with Garston. Aside from the town services, the garage participated in operating trunk services 301 (shared with Tring), 302 (Watford Heath–Hemel Hempstead) and 330/A (Hemel Hempstead–St Albans–Welwyn Garden City), as well as the aforementioned 347/A. A number of Merlins, introduced in LT days, plied some of the town services, whilst the Green Line operations and rural network inevitably featured members of the RF class.

A start was made on RT replacement in March 1972, when a number of RMCs arrived to take over operation of the 330/A group. Interworkings occasionally brought these surplus coaches to the 301, 302 and 312 and also to some of the myriad of town routes. Further RMCs arrived in October for route 312 but initially were placed on the 320 (Leverstock Green–Gadebridge) due to the problems of 'rowdyism' encountered on this service, the provision of platform doors being considered a definite pluspoint. After a few weeks, however, the vehicles were transferred to their intended route.

Operations at Hemel Hempstead were not immune to the whims of county councils. Conversion of its entire network to OMO was dictated ultimately by reductions in subsidy, although, to be fair, it had been one of London Country's stated aims at the company's inception. However, as the decade progressed and costs rose, such conversions assumed greater significance from the councils' point of view. Whereas Hertfordshire County Council ultimately became extremely supportive of public-transport initiatives (providing the sums added up), Bedfordshire took a different view. February 1972 saw the Studham–Dunstable section of route 337 withdrawn without replacement — Studham was the nearest point to the county boundary and thus the obvious place to terminate, in view of the lack of support from Bedfordshire CC. However, cutting off Dunstable — one of the main traffic objectives of the service — contrived to make the remainder of the operation totally uneconomic, and from July 1973 the service was withdrawn completely. Of course, as the decade progressed, further reductions of the

Almost begrudgingly, London Country conceded that the RF class would have a medium-term future within the fleet, as the type was suitable for OMO. Quite how the RF replacement programme would have progressed had the Country Area remained part of LT is one of those interesting 'might have beens', the outcome of which will never be known. RF replacement at Hemel Hempstead commenced in November 1975 with a token allocation of two MBs, and the last scheduled class members were replaced the following October. However, it would be May 1977 before the final examples departed from the area. May 1975 finds RF584 covering a traditional RF haunt, the 307, having arrived at Hemel Hempstead on a journey from Harpenden. *Colin Brown*

remaining rural network occurred, but a far more enlightened approach was adopted and very few areas subsequently lost their entire service.

Some fine-tuning of the Hemel Hempstead town network also occurred in July 1973, a number of services being simplified and suffix letters removed; interworkings were still extremely prolific, however! December 1973 saw the arrival of the garage's first Leyland Nationals, displacing the RFs on route 708. These Nationals were some of the first of the 10.3m batches and, although still basically buses, at least had seats covered in moquette rather than vinyl. As elsewhere, they were eventually replaced with Suburban Coach versions, in this case in March 1975.

Of all London Country garages, it was perhaps Hemel Hempstead which had the greatest difficulty in allocating the correct vehicle to the correct duty. Vehicle shortages certainly played a significant part in preventing correct allocations, but the conversion of routes from one type to another when sufficient vehicles of the proposed type were simply unavailable was another major factor. Crew-bus allocation was thus extremely fluid, from June 1974 right through until the final demise of crew operation in September 1978. From November 1975 the same problem affected the OMO fleet, but physical restrictions on certain routes precluded complete interchangeability of vehicle types.

The crew-bus situation took a bizarre twist in June 1974, when two additional RMLs were allocated for conversion from RT and RMC operation of a number of journeys on the many works and town services. Two RMLs were indeed transferred in, being employed mainly to cover for Hemel's non-existent RML allocation on route 347/A. There was now a scheduled requirement for four RMLs, but only three of the type were allocated, the shortfall being made up by the previous incumbents! The OMO conversion of routes 301 and 302 in May 1975, although displacing all of the remaining RT types, brought little stability (in terms of vehicle allocation) to the remaining crew work. A number of RTs had already been replaced, however, thanks to the arrival in March of Suburban Coach Nationals on the 708. The displaced buses had simply remained and were used in the ensuing period as crew-operated vehicles. The May OMO conversions also included many of the works services, and the vast majority now featured farebox operation with Leyland Nationals. Also to cease at the same time was scheduled RML work, other than the two buses intended for the 347/A. One RML had already moved out prematurely (in March) upon the arrival of crew-operated Nationals, and only two RMLs remained. Unfortunately one of these, RML2307, suffered mechanical failure and took an enforced summer break at Garston, where repairs were eventually effected. Hemel Hempstead therefore possessed only one RML for its share of the 347, the shortfall being made up by an RMC. Crew work also remained on the 312 and 330 allocations. In addition there were some peak-hour and lunchtime trips on the 301/302, which services also featured a handful of journeys worked by Garston; although scheduled for an RML, shortages dictated that, 99% of the time, the Garston workings were maintained by an RT. A further attempt was

October 1972 saw the official conversion of the majority of Hemel Hempstead's route 312 from RT to RMC operation. Initially, however, the latter were employed on the 320, a local town service that was suffering problems from some of the local 'lowlife' that crews regularly encountered *en route*, the provision of vehicles fitted with platform doors being a preferred option. By April 1974 the situation (vehicle-wise, at any rate) had stabilised, and the RMCs were regularly employed on their intended route. RMC1463 heads for Berkhamsted on route 312. *Steve Fennell*

The 320 retained its RTs until OMO conversion in May 1975. Here RT3118 heads away from Hemel Hempstead town centre in April 1974. *Steve Fennell*

made to increase the RML allocation at Hemel Hempstead in August, when the two RMCs allocated to the 312 were replaced on paper by RMLs, but, despite the return of RML2307 in September (for just a few weeks), Hemel Hempstead still possessed just one such bus to cover four allocated workings. In January 1976 even this was transferred out, and none of the longer Routemasters returned until the following September; as previously, it fell to an unofficial allocation of RMCs to make up the shortfall.

Replacement of the garage's last RFs was just as fraught — and just as confusing. November 1975 saw the arrival of two MBs to commence conversion of route 322 (Watford Junction–Hemel Hempstead). The drivers refused to accept dual-door vehicles on this service, however, and almost immediately they were transferred to the 301/302, the displaced Nationals taking up duties on the 322. This situation was maintained until May 1976, when further Merlins arrived for a partial conversion of routes 307/317 (Hemel Hempstead–Harpenden/Berkhamsted) and 352 (Hemel Hempstead–Sarratt–Watford). Further examples for the 322 arrived at the same time, but, as with previous plans to operate on this route, it simply didn't happen. Throughout the summer of 1976 the allocation of OMO vehicles was extremely fluid and bore little relation to what was actually scheduled. The MBs were spread throughout all the garage's single-deck services but were kept away from the 322, whilst the Nationals were similarly spread but made up the entire allocation on the 322. Added to this, a small number of RFs still remained, and these could also be seen on the full range of services. However, they tended to be kept away (not always successfully) from the 301 and 302! On paper, the last RFs were replaced by SNBs in October, but two could still be found at Hemel Hempstead in 1977, being withdrawn following CoF expiry in March and May. The final example, RF168, was transferred in from Garston only in January 1977.

A complete recasting of the town services occurred from January 1977, with a new series of routes numbered in the 'H' series. At the same time, the opportunity was taken to remove all MB work from the schedules. It was intended that the town network be wholly MBS-operated, but, despite the arrival of further examples from Windsor in exchange for some of the resident MBs, a shortfall still occurred, and a number of new Leyland Nationals were allocated to assist. As for the MBs, although displaced on paper, the majority remained, and it was not until July that the last three moved on.

The year 1977 would also see a further reduction in crew operation. The introduction in January of revised town services saw the Town Centre–Grove Hill section of the 312 replaced by one of the new 'H' routes, and an RML moved from Hemel Hempstead to Harlow as a consequence. Hemel Hempstead had renewed its acquaintance with RMLs late the previous year when two examples had actually made it from Garston in September and November respectively, but, again, intentions were not fulfilled, and the sole remaining example also moved back to Garston in March, leaving Hemel's two-bus share of the 347 back in the hands of RMCs.

Two interesting crew workings resulted from the January changes, as the new H13 (Railway Station–Swallowdale Lane) and H15 (Apsley Mills–Leverstock Green) both had isolated scheduled RMC workings. That on the H13 was a morning-peak facility, whilst that on the H15 ran during the afternoon period and surprisingly was booked for a St Albans vehicle! Such oddities were destined to be short-lived, however, as from November 1977 both these and route 330 were converted to OMO with the (by now) usual Leyland Nationals. Thus it fell to the 347/A to provide the last vestige of crew work at Hemel Hempstead. Officially allocated RMLs, the last of which had departed in March 1977, the service was maintained solely by RMCs. Five examples remained allocated, creating the potential for crew buses to appear on OMO workings. A regular operation at the time was the use of an RMC on the H1 (Moor End–Gadebridge circular), and appearances continued on a semi-regular basis until June 1978, when three of the RMCs were transferred away. Only RMC1454/87 remained, surviving until September, when replacements in the form of a small batch of new Atlanteans arrived to allow OMO conversion and also to provide a measure of additional capacity on some of the peak-hour 'H' services.

The last vehicles to maintain a London Transport influence at Hemel Hempstead were the surviving Merlins. At the introduction of the 'H' scheme in January 1977 it was planned that the standard vehicle for town-service work would be the MBS. However, in a somewhat abrupt U-turn, this decision was reversed, and from April further Nationals started to replace the remaining Merlins. Coinciding with the closure of Tring garage and the associated changes at Hemel Hempstead, the 301/302 was considered a suitable home for surplus 11.3m Nationals, the displaced 10.3m examples being fitted with fareboxes and transferred to town work. From April just four MBSs remained scheduled, so somewhat surprising was the fact that it took over 18 months to retire them from service. As late as September 1978 there was still a scheduled requirement for two such buses, and it was not until December that year that the last survivors, MBS407/36, were finally delicensed.

Despite Routemaster conversion in March 1972, Hemel Hempstead's RTs were still fairly frequent visitors to route 330 until such time as the last examples were replaced at HH in May 1975. RT3119 is seen at a strangely deserted Welwyn Garden City in March 1973. *Steve Fennell*

Garston

MY first visit to Garston garage was during January 1969. Then still under London Transport jurisdiction, it was on my list of places to visit because it was used to store large numbers of new AEC Merlins intended for Country Area service. That first visit did not disappoint: the rumoured Merlins were indeed present, but what struck me at the time was the garage's size and the number of vehicles of many different types to be found within; Country Area garages tended to be much smaller than those in the Central Area, but Garston bucked the trend and also had considerable operational variety, which continued well into London Country days.

In LT days a start had been made on reducing the amount of crew work at Garston, with the introduction of a sizeable number of Merlins during the spring of 1969. However, lack of suitable vehicles precluded further OMO conversions, and thus considerable crew work remained. It was not until July 1972, following delivery of suitable vehicles, that London Country instigated a large OMO conversion which replaced the majority of the garage's remaining RTs, new Leyland Atlanteans taking over operation of routes 321 (Uxbridge–Watford–St Albans–Luton), 385/A (Rickmansworth–Watford–Garston) and express service 803 (Maple Cross–Watford–St Albans–Welwyn Garden City). A few RTs remained, ostensibly covering the diminutive Garston allocation on routes 301/302, as well as the 345 (Napsbury Hospital–Bushey Station) and assorted odd trips on the many schools services which proliferated in the area — the operational diversity of the handful of survivors was considerable.

RTs aside, the remaining crew work was in the hands of RMLs, which plied their trade on routes 306/A (Leavesden–Watford–Borehamwood–New Barnet), 311 (Leavesden–Watford–Shenley) and 347/A (Uxbridge–Watford–Hemel Hempstead). Originally it was intended that further Atlanteans should be used to convert routes 306/311, but insufficient were available to permit conversion of both services, and it was considered impractical to convert one but not the other, due to the common routing shared by these services in the Watford area. Eventually the Atlanteans were deployed at Grays, and it was not until September 1976 that conductors on the 306/311 would be dispensed with. Once vehicle shortages manifested themselves from 1974 onwards, Garston always seemingly had more difficulty than most garages in providing sufficient vehicles for service. Worst affected was its RML fleet; indeed, by August 1975 Garston could muster only seven of an allocated 22 examples. Although London Country was very much at the back of the queue as far as the supply of Routemaster spare parts was concerned, the root of the problem could be traced back to a decision made in 1972 that Garston's entire fleet would receive recertification in *lieu* of full overhaul courtesy of London Transport's Aldenham Works. Although it was no

In November 1975 Garston garage received a mass influx of RMCs displaced from Dartford following the hiring of a batch of Leyland PD2s from Maidstone Corporation. Throughout the year, crew-bus availability at Garston had been dire, many of the garage's RMLs having fallen by the wayside awaiting spare parts; sadly, some of these buses were subsequently cannibalised to keep others going, and many never saw service again. Garston had already been bailed out by the arrival of a large batch of RTs released from OMO conversions at Hemel Hempstead and Tring in May, these ironically arriving at the same time as Garston's last scheduled RTs were (officially) replaced. However, the arrival of the RMCs at long last allowed a full crew-bus allocation to be operated, and all remained at Garston until September 1976, when OMO conversion of routes 306 and 311 permitted their return to Dartford. For the remainder of 1975 and throughout 1976, therefore, crew-bus operation at Garston was extremely interesting, featuring RTs, RMCs and the incumbent RMLs. One evening in June 1976, RMC1457 passes Bushey Arches displaying blinds for route 306A. This was not, however, a scheduled 306A journey; while the bus had indeed worked that rare peak-hour variation that morning, no crew had bothered to change the blinds back to the correct 306 display during the course of the day. *Steve Fennell*

doubt felt to be the best option at the time, the folly of this decision became apparent in subsequent years: as it proved impossible to keep them serviceable, many of Garston's RMLs were delicensed during 1975, some never to carry passengers again.

A major OMO conversion occurred at Garston garage in July 1972, when new Atlanteans replaced RTs on routes 321/385/A and 803. This conversion put paid to the vast majority of Garston's sizeable RT fleet, but in true London Country fashion a few lingered on, both on a scheduled and unscheduled basis, the last examples finally being withdrawn in April 1977. Soon after entry into service, AN58 is seen at Rickmansworth on the newly converted 385 route. These Atlanteans were impressive if somewhat ponderous vehicles, and the image portrayed by their arrival was no doubt aided by the attractive livery carried when new. The lack of a complete original example in preservation is a great shame, as they transformed the face of many areas of the London Country empire and represented an important facet of the company's history. *Colin Brown*

The 347/A represented a long-standing RML operation, although in latter days vehicle allocations tended to be a little fluid as shortages dictated the operation of a number of RMC and RT types. These services represented the last scheduled crew work from Garston garage, and OMO conversion in the form of new Atlanteans occurred from September 1978. Some years earlier, in March 1973, RML2435 stands at Uxbridge station prior to undertaking the long cross-country journey to Hemel Hempstead. *Colin Brown*

Unconfirmed at the time but suspected as an option for the future was the purchase of London Country's Routemasters by London Transport. The first were reacquired by LT in December 1977 and in the fullness of time the vast majority returned to LT ownership. However, some had been heavily cannibalised, and, following an analysis of its acquisitions, LT despatched two RMCs, two RCLs and 17 RMLs to a dealer in South Yorkshire for scrap, with such spare parts as remained being returned. Suffice to say the purchase of these vehicles by LT was fraught with problems; at one stage London Country appeared to lose patience with the demands placed upon it by LT and in March 1979 sold a batch of 17 for scrap. This action appeared to have the desired effect, in that LT immediately took steps to prevent the buses from being broken up, and, although a further two RMLs did slip through the net and were scrapped, further negotiations between the two organisations appeared to be much more fruitful. Whether coincidental or not, of the 19 RMLs scrapped, eight originated from Garston's original batch!

Apart from the aforementioned Atlanteans, Garston's OMO vehicle requirements were met by both MB- and MBS-type Merlins and a handful of RFs. Routes 318 (Watford–Abbots Langley), 335 (Watford–Windsor), 346/A (Kingswood–Watford–South Oxhey) and 352 (Watford–Bucks Hill/Hemel Hempstead) were operated primarily by Merlins, although RFs did play a minority role on the 352. RF operation involved routes 309 (Chorleywood–Harefield) and the 319 group — a complicated network of infrequent services operating within the Watford, Abbots Langley and Sarratt triangle and featuring suffixes from A to D! Also RF-operated was Garston's share of route 719 (Hemel Hempstead–London–Wrotham).

Garston garage was also home to the last two operational members of the GS class. These diminutive but appealing vehicles survived for operation on route 336A (Rickmansworth–Loudwater Village), upon which physical restrictions precluded the use of a larger vehicle. GS33 and GS42 were the survivors of a once 84-strong fleet intended for use on lightly trafficked rural services. For many years the operation of the 336A was worked from an outstation at Loudwater Village, the vehicle returning to Garston only once a week for maintenance; the driver used to pay in his takings on a daily basis at Rickmansworth station. Under normal circumstances the two surviving GSs worked alternate weeks, but towards the end GS42 seemed to be the favoured vehicle. The route was hopelessly uneconomic, and, following the retirement of the regular driver in 1971, the bus had to operate to/from Garston each day to take up service. Not surprisingly, this additional cost did nothing to prolong the route's existence, and it was withdrawn without replacement in March 1972. The last day of operation was Friday 29th, and from late afternoon onwards, probably for the first time ever, the service was duplicated. Both GSs (GS42 as service bus, with GS33 duplicating) became increasingly busy as the last journey approached, and the last actual service journey was somewhat protracted, various 'laps of honour' of Loudwater being undertaken as each bus vied to be the last one in. In the event GS42 achieved fame as the very last London Country GS to operate in service and, after performing the last journey on the 336A, concluded the process by running (albeit unofficially) as an additional 309 between Rickmansworth and Garston garage.

The Watford area also featured a complicated network of schools services, operated by all manner of different vehicle

April 1975 finds RT3752 covering for an RML on route 311 at Leavesden Works. Such substitutions were fairly common at the time, a number of Garston's RMLs being incapacitated. This particular vehicle was then unique in carrying the interim mid-green livery, following overhaul in April 1972, and would be Garston's last operational RT, surviving in service until 13 April 1977. *Mike Harris*

A memorable day was Friday 29 March 1972, when London Country said farewell to its last operational GS vehicles. Nominally a one-bus allocation, route 336A was duplicated during the final day of operation, probably for the first time ever. GS42 was destined to be the last to see service and, after completing the last 336A journey, was used as an unscheduled extra on route 309 between Rickmansworth and Garston. It is pictured at Rickmansworth station prior to undertaking this final working back to Garston garage. *Steve Fennell*

A handful of journeys on routes 301/302 were operated by Garston garage. This allocation comprised just one bus and included the two daily journeys between Watford and Hemel Hempstead via the Watford bypass, numbered 301B. Although officially converted to RML operation in May 1975, appearances of the type were extremely rare, and the working in question — GR27 — was nearly always allocated an RT. One evening in July 1976, however, RMC1511 was used, being seen at Kings Langley on the evening-peak 301B journey.
Steve Fennell

types. Such services were suffixed variations of the 318 and 346 operation, but in truth some links with the parent route were extremely tenuous. Attempting to record these workings on film was often very frustrating, as there nearly always seemed to be a problem with the buses' displaying correct route information on the destination blinds. The behaviour of the clientèle could also be 'problematical', while the results of vehicle shortages were self-explanatory! However, if one was prepared to persevere then a visit to 'do the school buses' could be highly rewarding. The trick was to ascertain exactly what was running, ensure the correct blinds were set prior to the buses' leaving the garage and then adopt a low profile at a suitable point for photography along the line of route — all easier said than done!

It was undoubtedly the chronic shortage of crew buses that made the operations at Garston so interesting from 1975 onwards. The appalling availability of Garston's resident RML fleet has already been described, and, when revisions planned in conjunction with the OMO conversion of routes 301/302 at Hemel Hempstead and Tring in May 1975 involved the replacement of Garston's last RTs by further RMLs, it was obvious even to an outsider that this simply couldn't happen! On paper Garston's last RTs were replaced from 31 May, but in reality the majority of the RTs displaced from both Hemel Hempstead and Tring migrated to Garston, where they collectively provided the majority of the serviceable crew-bus allocation. Insufficient destination blinds were available for such a large influx, but after a few weeks, thanks to the efforts of some local enthusiasts, the situation improved dramatically, and such vehicles became a regular sight on all Garston's crew workings. In the past, RT substitutions had occurred mainly on the 347/A, with appearances on the 306/311 being considerably rarer, but that policy was impossible to implement with so few Routemasters available, and the RTs were freely interspersed. Further variety was provided in November by the arrival *en masse* of Dartford garage's RMC fleet. These had been replaced by a batch of hired Maidstone PD3s and brought yet another type of crew bus to Garston's services. RMCs had been fairly regular (if unpredictable) visitors to Garston since 1973 — indeed, an overall-advertisement vehicle for London &

Manchester Assurance, RMC1490, included Garston on its year-long tour of London Country garages — but this was the first time that a sizeable number had been allocated at any one time, at least since LT days.

The RMCs remained until September 1976, when, following OMO conversion of routes 306/311, they were returned to Dartford. New Leyland Nationals were provided for this conversion, which also included the replacement of remaining crew journeys on Garston's small allocation on routes 301/302 and the odd remaining crew work on route 318. Spare Nationals also made their presence felt on route 319 in substitution for RFs as a prelude to their allocation later that same month. With such an influx of vehicles fitted with three-track number blinds, the opportunity was taken to remove routes with suffix letters, and the plethora of school services were renumbered in the 830 series. Crew journeys existed on new routes 833 (Carpenders Park–St Michael's School) and 835 (Watford–Queens School–Bushey Station) — the former 346D and 385C respectively. Also renumbered was the 346A to 345, the former 345 becoming the 834. A further renumbering proposed but not implemented was that of the 347A to 357.

At the time of the September 1976 revisions, Garston still retained five RTs. Two were survivors from its original allocation, intended for replacement as long ago as May 1975, whilst the other three originated from the 301 conversion from the same period. A side-effect of the revisions was the reappearance of these RTs on routes 321 and 345/346, as well as more traditional employment covering for RMLs on the 347/A. No doubt it was considered unsuitable for crew substitutions to occur on a newly converted OMO service, but the reappearance of RTs on these OMO services after so many years was remarkable, to say the least; in the case of the 345/346 (under the previous guise of 346/A) regular crew operation had ended in the spring of 1969. The surviving RTs continued in service until their careers were terminated by CoF expiry, four — RT2779, 3530, 3636 and 3752 — lasting into 1977. Of these, both RT2779 and RT3530 expired in January, whilst the other two survived until April. The final one of all, RT3752, last operated on the 13th, covering a duty on route 321.

It was not until September 1978 that crew operation was eradicated. Throughout 1977 and into 1978, CoF expiry had caused the garage considerable difficulties in providing sufficient RMLs for service, and, upon closure of High Wycombe garage in October 1977, the latter's entire stock of RMLs made their way to Garston. Further examples arrived from Staines later in the year, and a number of RMCs also returned. New Atlanteans commenced delivery in July 1978 and almost immediately were pressed into service as crew buses on the 347/A. The date set for OMO conversion was 2 September and this duly went ahead as planned, with the 347A being re-numbered 348 (instead of 357, as originally intended). At first, insufficient Atlanteans were available for the full OMO service and a number of RMLs were retained, albeit only for a couple of weeks. Most surprisingly, these survivors were fitted with blinds for the 348, allowing their use on this service and in the process giving Garston the honour of operating the last 'new' Routemaster route within the company. The last day of unofficial crew working was 15 September, when RML2429/42/56 all saw service.

Backtracking to single-deck developments over the same period, January 1974 saw the arrival of 10.3m Leyland Nationals to replace the RFs on route 719. In the fullness of time the more refined Suburban Coach version took over such duties, but initially the standard bus-seated variety had to suffice. January 1977 witnessed the replacement of Garston's last RFs, operating on the 309, which route allegedly had physical restrictions precluding the use of the larger vehicles. Rather than allocate yet another vehicle type to Garston in the form of Bristol LHSs, the powers-that-be made the sensible decision to transfer the route to Amersham garage, which already had experience of operating the type. On paper, Garston's were the last scheduled RFs operating within the company, despite the fact that eight garages still accommodated the odd RF or two on an unscheduled basis. Initially Garston's three were moved away, only to return the following month as spares. CoF expiry finally brought about their demise, the last, RF200, being withdrawn in May.

Concurrent with removal of the remaining crew work was replacement of the garage's Merlin fleet with Leyland Nationals. Initially the vehicles were provided by a reduction in the special

GR27 again, this time in June 1976, featuring the more usual RT in the form of RT3636. Seen leaving Watford, the bus is working Garston's sole evening-peak journey on route 302. On arrival at Two Waters (Hemel Hempstead) the vehicle would return to Watford as a 301B (see RMC1511 above) before working some journeys between Watford and Abbots Langley on route 347. This particular working also fell victim to the OMO conversions of September 1976. *Steve Fennell*

school services, but from October 1978 new deliveries enabled the last Merlins to be replaced — on paper. In practice Garston retained one MB and five MBSs as spare vehicles, but they saw little use other than on the Saturdays-only special pre-Christmas Watford Shopperbus service. All bar one were withdrawn in January 1979; MBS278 just survived into February, its last day of operation believed to have been the 4th.

Route 319, along with the A, B, C and D variations, was another long-standing RF route, with both Garston and Hemel Hempstead garages having a stake in its operation. Service reductions and restructuring eventually dispensed with the majority of the suffix workings, and, to aid the introduction of vehicles fitted with three-track number blinds, all surviving variations were simply numbered 319. RF700, the very last RF of all, spent its entire London Country career based at Garston and is seen here at Watford in July 1972. *Peter Graves*

St Albans

MY first visit to St Albans in London Country days was shortly before the intorduction of the AEC Swifts acquired from South Wales Transport. Classified SMW, a couple of these vehicles were at St Albans for training purposes, and I well remember my thoughts at the time when I discovered that three-track number blinds were fitted. That alone made them appear (to me, at least) totally alien, and somewhat naïvely I assumed that they would be modified to 'the normal specification' prior to entry into service. They weren't, of course, and over the next few years such features became very much accepted practice on new deliveries. The first few SMWs entered service in October 1971, initially carrying conductors, whilst January 1972 saw them take over routes 338 (St Albans–Radlett), 342/343 (London Colney/Brookmans Park–St Albans–Markyate–Dunstable) and 361 (St Albans–How Wood Estate). RTs were displaced, and just two months later RMCs arrived from Addlestone to finish the job when routes 330/A (Hemel Hempstead–St Albans–Welwyn Garden City) and the minority St Albans share of the 341 (St Albans–Hatfield–Hertford) lost their RTs and received these displaced Green Line vehicles.

St Albans also possessed some MBSs, which were used on local cross-city services, whilst the majority of the remaining OMO work fell to the ubiquitous RF. An interesting set of vehicle transfers took place during June 1972, when St Albans' fleet of bus-style RFs was exchanged with Dunton Green's modernised examples, to avoid the need for each garage to stock both sets of parts. Commendable though this exchange was, subsequent vehicle shortages put paid to any further initiatives of this nature, although, to the best of my knowledge, St Albans never operated another bus-style RF. RFs also operated the remnants of Green Line routes 712/713 (St Albans–London–Dorking), whilst some of the first of the new RP

coaches had arrived in December 1971 and took up residence on route 727 (Luton–Watford–Heathrow–Kingston–Gatwick–Crawley). These had replaced the original 1965 batch of Reliances (RC class), which themselves had arrived at St Albans only the previous August.

October 1973 saw the arrival of Bristol LHSs to commence RF replacement, primarily on routes 304 (Radlett–St Albans–Hitchin), 355 (Borehamwood–St Albans–Harpenden) and 382 (St Albans–Codicote). These vehicles had commenced delivery the previous June, but their entry into service was delayed due to the need for all drivers to be in possession of a full Class 1 (manual) PSV licence. They were not particularly well received at St Albans (a recurring theme, wherever they were allocated), not least due to their appalling ride and manual transmission! These first arrivals were classified BL and were constructed to an overall width of 8ft; later deliveries acknowledged the fact that physical problems could (and did) arise with allocation to certain services and were only 7ft 6in wide.

Leyland Nationals appeared from April 1974 and put paid to the remaining RFs on routes 712/713 and 313 (St Albans–Potters Bar–Enfield). The situation at St Albans really highlighted the problems inherent with running so many different vehicle types at the same garage; it now possessed BLs, MBSs, RPs, SMWs, SNBs and SNCs. In true London Country tradition, odd RFs still appeared, and perhaps the most diplomatic description to apply to the OMO workings at St Albans was that vehicle allocation was now extremely fluid! Reliability and consequently availability was taking its toll, and although each vehicle working was allocated a specific type, it simply wasn't happening. Compounding the problems was the fact that, in general, destination blinds on specific types catered only for the routes upon which they were booked to run, and blank screens and hand-written paper labels soon became a familiar sight in

For those used to the exacting standards adopted by London Transport, the arrival in 1971 of SMWs with provincial-standard three-track number blinds took some getting used to. Two varieties arrived: a batch of three dual-door Marshall-bodied examples, which entered service at Crawley garage, and a batch of 12 Willowbrook-bodied single-door examples, which saw service at St Albans. A number of the latter entered service in October 1971 and comprised a partial allocation on routes 338/343/358/361, replacing RTs. The balance entered service the following January and, along with a few RF workings, allowed OMO conversion of the aforementioned group of services. The October batch initially entered service as crew-operated buses, but the following January the luxury of conductors was dispensed with and all operated as OMO vehicles. May 1972 finds SMW6 covering a duty on route 343. *Colin Brown*

Aside from the regular operation on route 330, the only crew working at St Albans was a single morning-peak round-trip between St Albans, Markyate and Hatfield on route 343. In June 1975 RMC1504 is seen at Redbourne on what was the sole double-deck working on this service. This trip would survive until the end of crew working at St Albans garage in November 1977. *Steve Fennell*

the city — a far cry from the standards inherited in 1970, but sadly not unique to St Albans. Needless to say, such values failed to inspire, and, despite the attraction of the 330/A RMC allocation, my visits to St Albans rapidly decreased. There was, however, one jewel in the crown, and that was the morning peak RMC journey on route 343. Despite vehicle shortages, this was a fairly reliable performer, and I did make a number of expeditions to capture it on film. Rather frustratingly on two of the occasions I made the effort it was the same vehicle — RMC1504 — which was allocated. I well remember the last instance I and two colleagues captured this working on film sometime in May 1977. A car was available, and the plan was to drive to Hemel Hempstead and take the RMC journey on route H13. A somewhat fast drive to Markyate then followed to intercept the 343, before we headed off, again at high speed, to photograph the Hatfield RMC working on the 844. This plan was fraught with problems, not least the possibility of getting pulled for speeding, but suffice to say it worked for me on at least two occasions! Such was the decline in 'interesting' operational variety during this period that such expeditions were often planned around making the most of a worsening situation.

All good things come to an end, and November 1977 saw the cessation of crew operation at St Albans. Replacement was total, with no odd RMCs staying on after the conversion date; further SNBs were called upon to provide the necessary means of replacement. However, further juggling of single-deck resources continued to provide considerable variety right through to 1980,

when efforts were made to standardise vehicle types. The operating staff at St Albans were far from happy about the use of MBS vehicles on 'country' services (primarily the 313), to which such vehicles had now been allocated. Despite protestations, the problem was still simmering and ultimately led to unofficial strike action in January 1979. Following discussions with the trade unions the use of SMs was agreed, and four such vehicles — SM120, 454/7/85 — were taken out of storage and allocated to route 313. SM120 was subsequently found to be defective and returned whence it came, but the remaining three were rather more enduring and survived at St Albans until March 1981. Some weeks after their arrival they were reallocated from the 313 to local city services, but such allocations were still relatively academic, and a free-for-all still existed as far as day-to-day operational requirements were concerned. Further SNBs consigned the MBS fleet to history by September 1979, leaving just the three recently arrived SMs as the last vehicles of LT specification at the garage. When these SMs were finally withdrawn in March 1981 they were not only the last buses of LT specification to operate from St Albans but also amongst the last of their type to operate for the company, being outlasted by only a few weeks by three survivors at Addlestone.

Many thought that after the January 1970 split the use of red vehicles on Country Area routes would pass into history. Nothing could have been further from reality, however, witness the use of five loaned red crew RFs (the last of which were returned to LT in February 1971), some red XAs at East Grinstead (pending repaint) and the well-documented hire of over 40 LT Merlins (from June 1974). One fairly regular but unpredictable operation was the appearance of Central RFs on Green Line 727, but generally this practice seemed to die out towards the end of 1974. On one of the last occasions that such an operation occurred, RF426 is seen at St Albans garage, having taken over from an ailing RP at Kingston, during September 1974. *Steve Fennell*

Luton

LUTON garage had the misfortune to be the first to be closed under London Country management. Circumstances dictated, however, that it would not be the last, and, looking back, one can appreciate that both London Country and Bedfordshire County Council failed to realise the full implications of the relatively recent requirement for public-transport funding. Such subsidies were very much in their infancy however, and in years to come, although the underlying trend was one of retrenchment, many fruitful negotiations were undertaken between the company and the county councils to provide adequate and affordable levels of rural bus operation. Unfortunately, attitudes prevailing at the time were not conducive to such negotiations.

It had to be accepted that many of London Country's rural routes were giving serious cause for concern as running costs escalated and revenue shrank, and there was much speculation concerning London Country's stance on these operations. In 1971 the company issued a statement along the lines that 'the County Councils have received three months' formal

The first garage closure instigated by London Country was at Luton, where service reductions had rendered the local garage hopelessly uneconomic to operate. Here the signs come down from above the garage entrance on Friday 28 January 1977, its last day as an operational garage. *Steve Fennell*

notification of the Company's intention to withdraw loss-making rural routes but have been invited by the Company to enter into discussions on the possibility of making a grant for any of the routes that they wish to be retained…'. Bedfordshire County Council declined to make any such subsidy towards services, and the result was the decimation of London Country's rural network in that county. February 1972 saw the withdrawal of a considerable chunk of the RF-operated network from Luton. Services dispensed with included route 337 (Hemel Hempstead– Dunstable) between Studham — the nearest point to the Bedfordshire/Hertfordshire boundary — and Dunstable and routes 343A (Dunstable–Studham) and 352 (Dunstable–Dagnall). The Markyate–Kensworth–Studham/Whipsnade Zoo section of the 364A also disappeared, whilst the parent 364 (Hitchin–Luton– Markyate) was re-routed away from Woodside Village. Local journeys within Bedfordshire were not permitted, although passengers could still travel into Bedfordshire from points outside the county boundary. Such cuts threatened the long-term existence of the 337 and 364, and their complete withdrawal in July 1973 would come as no real surprise.

July 1972 saw a further round of operating economies affecting operations from Luton, although the main event was the conversion of route 321 (Luton–St Albans–Watford–Uxbridge) to OMO, with new AN-class Leyland Atlanteans replacing RTs. The 321 operation was shared with Garston and

represented a significant proportion of work remaining at Luton at the time. Economies were also made to routes 360 (Luton–Caddington–Dunstable) and 364, whereby the Sunday service on each was converted to OMO RF. The Sunday crew operation of route 364 had been the result of scheduling efficiency rather than any justification on traffic grounds; indeed, the Sunday operation covered only the Luton–Markyate section, and it was surprising that such pockets of hopelessly uneconomic activity had not been dealt with earlier. Further reductions saw the withdrawal of the Mon-Sat service on route 365 (Luton–Wheathampstead–St Albans), with the limited-stop service 366 (Luton–Welwyn Garden City) being altered to cover all stopping-points on common sections of route. The Sunday service on the 365 survived a little longer, but that too succumbed in July 1973.

The year 1974 dawned with Luton mustering only a 15-vehicle run-out — a reduction of 10 since London Country's inception — and, considering the economic circumstances of the company's operations, it is perhaps surprising that the garage would last another three years before closure. Surviving services were the 321, 360, 366 and Green Line 714 (Luton–London–Dorking), operated with ANs, RTs, RFs and SNCs respectively. Somewhat unexpected was the introduction in July 1975 of a new Fridays and Saturdays service between Codicote and Luton which revived the 365 number; this was a very short-notice replacement for a service provided by Jey-son Coaches which had ceased operation, and was the last to be introduced featuring RF vehicles, the resources being made available by the withdrawal of the Caddington–Dunstable section of service 360. More surprising was the fact that the Saturday operation was crew-operated, again to facilitate efficient rostering.

Although the writing was quite clearly on the wall, replace-ment of former LT vehicles was still undertaken. In January 1976 two new SNBs replaced the two surviving RFs — RF68 and RF586; crew-operated Nationals thus saw service on the recently introduced 365 route. Despite a partial 'paper' replacement in May, two RTs — RT3631/6 — survived until September, although the former was delicensed from July but resurrected briefly in September before being swiftly despatched to Tring, surprisingly for Green Line work. RT3530 was loaned from Garston for a few days in October but seemingly saw little use and was returned the same month. The final few weeks of crew operation on route 360 were thus undertaken by Leyland Nationals until December, when both this route and the 365 were transferred to United Counties in advance of closure of the garage due to staffing difficulties, the last day of service being Friday 28 January 1977. The small amount of bus work remaining was transferred to Garston (route 321) and Hatfield (366) garages. Green Line work was transferred to St Albans, but the opportunity was taken to revise completely the London–St Albans–Luton Green Line corridor. New AEC Reliances with purpose-built coach bodywork were a strong marketing feature of the revised 707/717 operation, which replaced the northern sections of routes 712/713/714 and signified the start of the much-acclaimed revamp of the Green Line network.

Stevenage

IN May 1969 Stevenage New Town had been the subject of a Department of the Environment report which opined that the needs of the still growing town would be better served by a high-quality bus service than by further highway expenditure. Such ideas were then quite radical and indeed, many years ahead of their time. Although the resultant experiment was seen through with great success and led to a significant increase in bus ridership, seemingly much of what was learned appears to have been ignored or forgotten over the ensuing years. No-one can deny that a high-frequency, low-priced, reliable bus service attracts custom; that has been proven time and time again, notably with use of high-frequency minibus schemes throughout the country in the early days of deregulation. Where such schemes were (and still are) badly let down is by the generally lethargic attitude to the provision (and subsequent effective enforcement) of bus-priority measures. Such measures should really have kept pace with road traffic growth over the last 30 years, but unfortunately there is now much catching-up to do. It would be extremely interesting to compare today's passenger-ridership figures over the Chells–Stevenage corridor with those from 1971. I think I can guess the result, but I would dearly love to be proven wrong!

The so-called 'Better Bus Service' experiments began on 29 December 1969 — three days prior to the London Country takeover — with the introduction of the Blue Arrow service between the Chells area and neighbouring industrial estates. Principles of the service included journeys based around factory start/finish times and flexibility in terms of pick-up/set-down points — buses did not serve conventional stopping-points but stopped wherever it was convenient and safe to do so. Also a part of the marketing was the provision of a guaranteed seat — passengers were pre-booked on individually timed buses and all

carried season tickets, normal point-to-point fares not being available. The Blue Arrow service introduced double-deck OMO to London Country, although technically (on a Monday morning, at least) the service was crew-operated, as a courier was carried on each journey to issue season tickets! The vehicles used were three XF Fleetlines, repainted in an eye-catching blue and silver and bearing London Country fleetnames from the first day of operation. Although they appeared to display route numbers — A1 and A2 — these were used merely to identify particular journeys, so that season-ticket holders would recognise the journey upon which they were booked to travel. Ever the optimist, London Transport had decreed that the blinds should carry 'numbers' from A1 to A6, allowing for a considerable expansion of service should the need arise. Subsequent events overtook the Blue Arrow concept, but it nevertheless set the scene for further experiments within the Stevenage New Town area.

The existing route network inherited by London Country comprised an extremely complicated pattern of RT-operated town services. Route numbers appeared to be duplicated in some cases, and, to add to the disorder, a number of 'A' and 'B' suffixes were used to denote certain variations, but, if every single variation had been treated in the same manner, there would have been insufficient letters in the alphabet! A small number of RFs operated the rural network, primarily routes 383 (Hitchin–Weston), 384/B (Letchworth–Stevenage–Hertford) and 807 (Stevenage–Weston–Letchworth), whilst five RMCs were provided for Green Line 716/A.

During early 1971 SM144 was displayed within the town centre in a dual livery, one side being painted canary yellow and Lincoln green whilst the other was canary yellow and Oxford blue. The purpose of the exercise was to gauge public opinion

A practice reintroduced by London Country was the operation of tours and excursions using its own vehicles; problems in LT days had seen most private-hire work (other than expeditions for garages' Sports & Social clubs) sub-contracted. Seen at Stevenage bus garage in September 1971, almost-new SM465, a Hatfield vehicle, is all set for an afternoon excursion to Heathrow Airport. At the time, these Swifts were the newest vehicles in the fleet and undertook a fair amount of excursion work. *Steve Fennell*

The Stevenage town network inherited by London Country comprised an extremely complicated group of RT-operated services. Route numbers appeared to be duplicated in some cases, and, adding to the disorder, a number of 'A' and 'B' suffixes were used to denote certain variations. The introduction of the first 'Superbus' service in the town from July 1971 saw the replacement of the Chells–Bus Station–Industrial Area service, numbered 809. However, in a manner seemingly typical of service provision in the New Towns, from the same date a new 809 was introduced, serving the St Nicholas area. In August 1971 RT4038 waits at Stevenage bus station on this newly introduced service. This 'new' 809 would be fairly short-lived, being amalgamated into the Superbus network in September 1972, but at the time of the photograph it was merely a one-bus RT operation.
Colin Brown

London Country's very first Leyland Nationals entered service at Stevenage in September 1972 and represented 'the shape of things to come'; London Country would eventually become the largest operator of the type. Only the first 70 were constructed to 11.3m length, all subsequent deliveries being of the shorter 10.3m variant, and most of the early longer models were destined for a relatively short life with LCBS. Just a few weeks after entry into service, LN1 is seen at Stevenage bus station undertaking Superbus work on the original Chells service, now numbered SB1 following the introduction of the St Nicholas service numbered SB2.
Colin Brown

as to the preferred choice of livery for the next stage of the 'Better Bus' experiments. When I stumbled across it, almost by accident one afternoon at Stevenage, it took me quite by surprise. I recall finding it quite bizarre, and remember being asked by a surveyor which colour scheme I preferred. I seem to recall that my answer of Lincoln green with a yellow waistband was not what he wanted!

Phase One of the experiment commenced on 20 March 1971, when traditional-liveried Swifts made their mark on route 809 (Chells–Bus Station–Industrial Area). The conversion featured traditional pay-as-you-enter fare-collection methods and, despite the introduction of an improved frequency, was an unmitigated disaster, with late running and bunching playing havoc with the service. Just six weeks later, Phase Two was introduced and featured the use of fareboxes — the first time such revenue-collection methods had been tried by the company. Operation was vastly improved and paved the way for Phase Three.

On Saturday 31 July five new Swifts and two Scania/MCW Metro-Scanias — all adorned in canary yellow and Oxford blue — launched 'Superbus'. This was an immediate success, vindicating all those who had advocated the provision of such a service. Ridership improved rapidly, so much so that by October two further Swifts, both repainted yellow and blue, were added. Still usage increased, prompting the allocation of a further two buses in February 1972. One victim of the outstanding success of the operation was the Blue Arrow service. Due to the improved frequencies on offer, more and more people were choosing to travel by the new service, and in April 1972 the XFs were replaced by yellow-and-blue SMs, the capacity of which was more in keeping with demand. Three further Swifts were repainted as a means of replacement and had arrived by April. Also arriving the same month were two further Metro-Scanias. Inevitably, due to falling demand, the Blue Arrow service ceased altogether, the last day of operation being 1 September the same year.

Saturday 2 September 1972 saw the Stevenage–St Nicholas route receive the Superbus treatment, sufficient vehicles being available following the withdrawal of the Blue Arrow operation;

the St Nicholas Superbus service was numbered SB2, whilst the original (un-numbered) Chells route became the SB1. However, the highlight for some was the introduction in passenger service of the company's first Leyland National vehicles. LN1 and LN2 both received the by now familiar yellow-and-blue scheme and were followed by LN3 and LN4 in December. They replaced four Swifts, which reverted to standard colours following their arrival and were allocated elsewhere. Suffice to say a visit was undertaken shortly afterwards to sample these new vehicles, and it was an interesting experience.

Despite the attraction and novelty value of the expanding Superbus, 1972 saw considerable upheavals affect the remaining operations at Stevenage. Firstly, in March, new RPs replaced RMCs on routes 716/A. From a personal point of view this was a particularly sad loss, as the 716 ranked high amongst my favourites. Many was the occasion when, having spent the day exploring the northern extremities of London Country's empire, I would head for home courtesy of the long cross-London trip to Kingston on an RMC on the 716. There was something about a long journey on a coach Routemaster which was hard to define; in the evenings, especially, there was an atmosphere which was sadly lacking on the replacement RPs. Certainly an element of tradition was apparent, and many of the coach crews were extremely long-serving members of staff who had worked the Green Line for years. Vehicle shortages nevertheless ensured that the 716/A continued to witness occasional RMC operation. Normally such initiatives were the preserve of Hatfield garage, but in September 1975 RMC1496 arrived at Stevenage to cover shortages and for several weeks was used on an almost daily basis on the 716; surprisingly, perhaps, Stevenage managed to muster a complete front set of RMC destination blinds for it. Quite unexpectedly I encountered this vehicle at Stevenage bus station one Saturday afternoon, when it rolled in covering the last round trip that day to Addlestone. A rapid change of plan saw me ensconced within, but progress was extremely slow because of the need to stick to OMO timings. Conveniently, a road-traffic accident (in which we were not involved) caused a 15-minute

The Blue Arrow service was introduced during the final days of London Transport control of the Country Bus network, although the three XF-class Fleetlines selected for the operation carried London Country fleetnames from day one. This service was the forerunner of the highly successful Superbus operation, and its introduction marked the first stage of the various experiments introduced within the town for the provision of better bus services. XF6 is seen on display at Chells a few days prior to introduction, promoting the virtues of the new service.
Steve Fennell collection (photographer unknown)

The small class of Metro-Scania single-deckers was concentrated at Stevenage and used on Superbus work. Three were acquired from Hants & Dorset in exchange for a like number of 11.3m Leyland Nationals, following H&D's takeover of King Alfred, the well-known and respected Winchester independent. One of the former King Alfred vehicles, MS6, is seen near Chells on the original Stevenage Superbus service, now numbered SB1. *Steve Fennell*

delay just north of Welwyn Garden City and provided the necessary incentive for a faster journey, and from there onwards a little of the old magic returned. All the lost time had been regained by the time we reached Kingston, where I alighted outside the garage and watched the RMC disappear towards Addlestone. This turned out to be my last journey by Routemaster coach on a 716.

Following the expansion of Superbus, virtually the entire Stevenage town network was treated to OMO in October 1972. Farebox operation with new Atlanteans was the order of the day, but attempts to simplify the network only met with a limited amount of success. A very small amount of crew work was retained at peak times on routes 303 and a new 303C (Stevenage Industrial Estates–Bus Station–Hitchin), two RTs being retained for this purpose.

The momentum of so many service alterations in such a relatively short space of time clearly couldn't be maintained, and, following this major change, the Stevenage area settled down to a reasonable period of stability. Reductions in May 1976 to the Green Line 716/A released sufficient RPs to replace the remaining RTs and RFs. Most surprising was the use of these RPs as crew-operated vehicles on former RT workings on the 303/303C. This was not the end of double-deck crew operation at Stevenage, however, as in July 1977, following displacement by OMO conversion at Harlow, RML2354 arrived to help cover short-term problems with RP availability. During its stay it covered a crew working on the 303/303C until moving on in October to Hertford, where a greater need for its services had been identified.

January 1977 saw the Superbus influence spread to the Martins Wood area, through the conversion of routes 813/814. However, slightly different this time was the use of Atlanteans on these services, which were renumbered SB3. However, appealing as yellow-and-blue Atlanteans might have been, the buses concerned merely received large yellow-and-blue 'SB' vinyls between the decks. July saw the Atlanteans move to the SB2 and form a partial allocation on the SB1, the SB3 receiving the displaced single-deck types. Behind the scenes, a decision had also apparently been made concerning the future of the yellow-and-blue livery, as, around this time, SM496 returned from repaint in NBC leaf green and was subsequently adorned with the aforementioned 'SB' vinyls.

October saw an exchange of work with adjacent NBC operator United Counties, Hitchin local service 383 being

swapped for the latter's 82 route. This transformed itself into London Country 314, operating from Hitchin to Welwyn Garden City via Langley, Codicote, Welwyn and Ayot Green. At the same time, a joint operation numbered 44 was introduced to replace United Counties route 45 — which, the previous December, had itself replaced London Country's 365 route, operated from Luton garage! The 44 ran from Stevenage to Luton via Knebworth and Nup End before following the erstwhile 45/365 routeing. Operation was Thursdays, Fridays and Saturdays only.

The Metro-Scania vehicles were withdrawn in 1978. Ultimately a total of seven had been obtained, a further three having been sourced from Hants & Dorset, which had acquired them with the takeover of well-known Winchester independent King Alfred Motor Services. They were exchanged for three Leyland Nationals and logically ended up at Stevenage. Operating a small, non-standard class was always a problem, and the expense and difficulty of obtaining spare parts ultimately led to their downfall. The last two to see service, MS2 and MS4, were withdrawn in October and September respectively.

During 1979 further Leyland Nationals arrived to allow commencement of Atlantean overhauls and were subsequently freely mixed in service on town routes. They also made their mark on Superbus services, although by now, thanks to the abandonment of the distinctive livery, the special nature of such routes was gradually being eroded.

Superbus officially died in April 1980, when a major revision of town services saw a restructured network being numbered in the 'SB' series, 'SB' now standing for Stevenage Bus rather than Superbus. Such changes saw the removal from the garage of the final SMs, including those still remaining in yellow and blue. Also planned for removal was the small fleet of RPs which had been retained for the non-town-service work. Despite the best-laid plans, shortages of Atlanteans caused the retention of some Nationals on town work, and it was not until the end of May that sufficient ANs became available to allow the cascade programme to take effect. Shortly after the introduction of the new network, on 17 May, an Open Day was held at the garage. As an attraction, RT1018, still holding a valid CoF but normally to be found on training duties, was 'imported' for the day to operate circular tours of the area. This turned out to be the very last occasion when an RT carried passengers under the auspices of London Country Bus Services, although the bus would survive in LCBS ownership until sold for preservation in March 1981.

Hatfield

The 1970s was the decade of the overall advertisement bus, and most operators possessed examples of this new phenomenon. London Country's first such vehicle was RMC1516, which received this quite startling livery advertising the virtues of Welwyn Department Store. The bus spent most of its time on routes 341/B — perhaps surprising, given that neither served Welwyn Garden City — and is seen here at Hatfield market-place in June 1973.
Colin Brown

HATFIELD garage had the distinction of being one of the first to receive RMC vehicles solely for bus work. Routes 303/A (New Barnet–Hatfield–Welwyn Garden City–Stevenage–Hitchin) had received surplus coaches in LT days, and this practice continued under the new management. When I discovered that the 303/A were set for OMO conversion in February 1971, I decided that I ought to pay a visit and make one last trip by RMC on the route. I was a little miffed (sacrilege!) when an RT turned up, but I nevertheless took it to Stevenage (where I discovered the aforementioned SM144 on display). The vast majority of other 303s espied that day were also RTs, and it turned out that they were being used to provide cover for the RMCs, which had been dispersed to allow overhaul cover for the remainder of the fleet. I never did manage another RMC trip on the route, as conversion to SM went ahead as planned in February 1971. The RMCs were intended to move onto the 341/B (St Albans–Hatfield–Hertford/South Hatfield), but the conversion was a little half-hearted, as the intended vehicles were still being used for overhaul cover, albeit now for RCLs. A proportion of RTs remained therefore and it wasn't until January 1972 that sufficient vehicles were available to enable replacement.

The 303/A were fast routes but extremely busy at times and thus susceptible to traffic delays. Previous experiences of the route had revealed vehicles being driven extremely hard to maintain time, and a more unsuitable vehicle than the SM would have been hard to find; its small, high-revving engine was simply not designed for this type of operation. London Country seemingly had the same view, as the SM's reign on these services was relatively short; in February 1973 all moved to Addlestone, where they replaced (on paper) the last RFs at that garage. Higher-powered MB vehicles took over the 303/A following displacement on other Hatfield services by some of the first Leyland National buses to enter service with the company. These had been intended for Green Line use, but not surprisingly their dual-door layout was considered more suitable for bus work. As a point of interest, the dual-door National did not find favour with LCBS, and only the first 23 were built to this specification (and three of these were transferred to Hants & Dorset, in exchange for its three Metro-Scanias). Even the use of MBs was short-lived, however, as, from August, further new single-door 11.3m Leyland Nationals made their mark, the MBs moving on for RF replacement, this time at Dorking and Guildford. Use of the 11.3m National was considered problematic, and only the first 70 were delivered to this length; for subsequent batches the company standardised on single-door 10.3m vehicles.

Route restructuring made its presence felt in the Hatfield/ Welwyn Garden City area from February 1974, when the familiar 324/340 group of services were transformed into a series of routes numbered upwards from 840. Such route number sequences were part of a 'Master Plan' whereby local services in the northern area would be numbered in the 800s and those in the south in the 900s. Stevenage and Harlow already had 800-series routes, so it was logical that this number range should continue; the Hatfield area was the only place where numbers were actually changed before the scheme was abandoned. City services at St Albans came close to being numbered into the 820 series but in the end gained 'S' prefixes instead, while the Watford area subsequently gained routes in the 830 series. However, the latter exercise was undertaken merely to replace suffixes on a motley selection of low-frequency school and hospital routes so as to facilitate the introduction of vehicles with three-track number blinds and was not part of the original proposals, the original sequence for Watford being (I believe) upwards from 860 or 880.

Whereas Hatfield's OMO bus fleet was now predominantly Leyland National, RP-class Reliances and RMCs remained for Green Line and crew work respectively. The majority of the new 840-series routes still had the odd crew journey scheduled, although in three cases this was a single journey only and operated by the same bus. More enduring were the workings on the 840 (South Hatfield–Welwyn Garden City), 842 (Birchwood Estate–South Hatfield) and 844 (Welwyn Garden City Station–Queen Elizabeth II Hospital), all of which lasted until the end of crew operation in November 1977. One of Hatfield's RMCs

February 1974 saw a complete restructuring of the Hatfield/Welwyn Garden City town-service network, with services now numbered in the 84x series. Such numbering was part of a 'master plan' whereby local services within the northern area would receive 8xx numbers whilst those south of the Thames would be numbered 9xx. This scheme died in its infancy, however, and subsequent revisions saw letter-prefixed services introduced instead. However, the Welwyn scheme went ahead prior to the change of plan, and thus sights such as RMC1497 on route 842 at South Hatfield could be savoured. Just a handful of journeys on the 84x group were scheduled for crew operation, standard fare being the inevitable Leyland National. RMC1497 was one of just a handful of the type painted with grey (as opposed to white) relief. *Mike Harris*

Brand-new LNB69 stands at Stevenage bus station on the busy 303 service. One cannot fail to be impressed by the appearance of such a vehicle, but disappointment awaited anyone sampling the interior! However, these Nationals were far more suited to a service such as the 303 than were the underpowered Swifts that had introduced driver-only operation to the route back in February 1971. Perhaps the most suitable vehicle for such a journey would have been an RMC, but by this time such thoughts amounted merely to wishful thinking. *Colin Brown*

Thanks to availability problems with Merlins and Swifts, RPs made fairly frequent appearances on Hatfield's local bus operations. In early LCBS days the 324 was operated by Autofare MBS vehicles, but decimalisation in February 1971 saw all such services converted to conventioanl OMO. Interestingly, during the Autofare period, substitutions by other OMO vehicles were not permitted under existing trade-union agreements, and, if a shortage of MBSs arose, any sustitutions employed crew-operated vehicles. After removal of the Autofare equipment any OMO vehicle could be used, witness the use of RP45 on route 324 at the Great Ganett terminus of this service during October 1972. *The late J. G. S. Smith*

was none other than prototype Green Line Routemaster RMC4, which, despite having some quite lengthy periods off the road, was a fairly regular performer when licensed. Distinguishing features included a standard three-piece front route-number/destination screen (*à la* RMLs); uniquely among Country Area Routemasters, it also had plain front upper-deck windows. Less noticeable, but certainly 'distinguishing' to the operating staff, was its lack of power-assisted steering! In January 1975 it disappeared into London Transport's Chiswick Works for a somewhat prolonged overhaul, not emerging until July 1976! In the intervening 18 months, aside from the obvious repaint into corporate NBC garb, it had also received opening front upper-deck windows. Quite why, at such a late stage in its career, this modification was considered necessary is unclear — it had, after all, managed perfectly well since 1957!

As mentioned above, Hatfield's remaining scheduled crew operations, primarily on route 341, ceased in November 1977, when further Leyland Nationals — albeit the (by now) standard 10.3m version — were allocated. Even ignoring any personal loyalties, it was always doubtful whether 41-seat single-deck buses were really suitable for such routes. The official company line was that there was very little difference in overall capacity between the 57+5 standees of an RMC and the 41+19 standees of a National. However, those who travelled on a regular basis thought otherwise, and it would be a brave man who could say that such conversions did not, over time, cause a further swing away from public transport. At the time, new double-deck vehicles suitable for OMO were not available (London Country's vehicle orders comprising only single-deck buses), and such were the financial implications of retaining crew operation that single-decking in the short term was considered to be the only option. Subsequently, when new Atlanteans finally became available, many services subjected to single-deck conversion regained an upper deck, but the damage was done, and the cynics amongst us would say that this was

really a case of shutting the stable door after the horse had bolted! Route 341 would eventually revert to double-deck operation in April/May 1981.

In 1977 RMC availability had been poor, and a couple of redundant Harlow RMLs had arrived in April to assist. For whatever reason, they were not highly regarded, but they nevertheless saw a reasonable level of use, primarily in peak hours. These two buses stayed on after OMO conversion, as did a handful of RMCs, including RMC4, the latter even managing a return to former glories on 9 September 1978, when it operated on Green Line route 722 (London–Hitchin); this had replaced the northern leg of the 716 in January 1978 as part of the major surgery carried out on the Green Line network at the time. The RMLs departed in April 1978, but two of the incumbent RMCs were a little more resilient. RMC1512 finally departed in January 1979 for Swanley, where it would ultimately become the last to see stage-carriage service. The other survivor, not surprisingly, was RMC4, and this could be found in service until May, when its historic status was finally acknowledged and it was officially preserved by the company. Two further RMCs had made fleeting visits in March 1979, but their use was minimal and they lasted only a few weeks.

Further restructuring of the local bus network occurred in May 1978. The 840-series routes, themselves only a fairly recent innovation, were replaced by a series of G-suffix services, and the remaining crew buses (other than RMC4, which had a specially made route-number blind fitted) now displayed various hand-written notices for route details.

During the autumn of 1979 the original 11.3m dual-door Nationals started to suffer CoF expiry and their place was taken by the shorter variety, examples being purloined from around the fleet. In the event, the company decided against recertifying the dual-door examples, and in 1980 the first were sold to British Caledonian Airways, no takers apparently having been found for them within the National Bus Company.

Hertford

HERTFORD garage was another early user of downgraded RMCs, in February 1971 gaining a partial allocation on its share of routes 341/B, replacing RTs. As in the case of Hatfield, this was a somewhat lax affair, as the vehicles themselves were being used to cover for RMC repaints and subsequently for RCL overhauls. The situation only really stabilised upon the OMO conversion of the 310/A (Hertford–Hoddesdon–Enfield) and 715/A (Hertford–London–Guildford) in April 1972. A partial RMC 'bus' allocation was nevertheless maintained throughout the interim period, and interworkings allowed for a small (albeit unscheduled) degree of Routemaster operation on all of Hertford's crew workings, including the intended 341/B.

The main type at Hertford in early LCBS days was undoubtedly the RF. Thirty examples were allocated for a scheduled requirement of 27, and they formed the main allocation on an assortment of mainly rural services, as follows:

308	Hertford–Goffs Oak
327	Hertford–Nazeing Village
329	Hertford–Knebworth
331/A	Hertford–Buntingford
333/B	Hertford–Bengeo–Chapmore End/Ware Park
350/A	Bishops Stortford–Hertford–Potters Bar
351	Buntingford–Much Hadham
384/A	Hertford–Letchworth/Dane End (Allocation shared with Stevenage)
386	Hitchin–Stevenage–Buntingford–Bishops Stortford/Hertford (One journey operated by Stevenage)
388	Hertford–Welwyn Garden City
389	Ware local service
390	Stevenage–Hertford–Harlow–Sawbridgeworth (Allocation shared with Harlow and odd journeys by Stevenage)
393/A	Welwyn Garden City–Hertford–Harlow (Allocation shared with Harlow)

As was typical of the area, some of these services operated only a few journeys each day on certain days of the week. Inevitably some met an early demise as requests for council funding fell (initially, at least) on deaf ears. Early casualties of this policy were the 329 and 351, both withdrawn in August 1971, and the Bengeo–Chapmore End section of the 333, withdrawn in August 1972. Others suffered quite extensive reductions, but, conversely, crew journeys with double-deckers survived until 1976 to cover heavily loaded journeys on services such as the 331/A and 350/A. Eventual replacement, later in the decade, of the garage's RF fleet brought considerable variation to the rural network as many different vehicle types were used to effect replacement. Such variations increased as vehicle shortages worsened.

OMO conversion of the 310/A brought into service the first of London Country's new AN-class Atlanteans. Their livery matched the style first seen on the ex-Western Welsh Fleetlines introduced at Godstone two months earlier, and the original batches were very much 'LT' in details such as destination

The first of London Country's AN-class Atlanteans entered service on routes 310/A, concurrent with conversion of the last remaining RMC-operated Green Line route, the 715/A, to RP operation, as part of a large OMO scheme at Hertford in April 1972. Officially the garage's remaining RTs were replaced in one fell swoop, with the redundant Green Line RMCs providing the allocation on the small remaining proportion of crew work; RT3250 is seen near Ware in April 1972 on route 310, just a few days prior to OMO conversion. However, such was the reliability of the new vehicles that RTs and RMCs would continue to feature heavily in maintaining operations on an unscheduled basis on route 310/A. During 1977 a small number of RMLs arrived — the first time such vehicles had been based at Hertford — and these also saw regular operation on route 310, until April 1978. *Peter Graves*

displays. Subsequent deliveries, whilst retaining the same basic appearance, featured standard NBC three-track number blinds and one-piece destination screens, as well as the obligatory coat of leaf green.

The arrival of the Atlanteans at Hertford, coupled with the delivery at the same time of new RP-class Reliances for Green Line work, saw the removal of all remaining scheduled RT work at the garage. The surviving crew operations were now in the hands of RMCs and comprised the one-bus allocation on route 341 and the majority of workings on routes 395/A (Hertford–Ware). One RMC, however, was allocated to routes 350/A, and the operations of this one particular bus rate it high in the league of London Country's notable workings. Leaving Hertford at 06.35 (ish) in the morning, it operated to Bishops

Stortford via the extremely rural 350A routeing before returning via the equally bucolic 350 route. Morning's work over, it retired to Hertford garage until called upon later in the day to perform a return journey between Hertford and Buntingford over routes 331/A. This one example of crew operation epitomised the appeal of the country network at the time, yet, even then, such operations were regarded as extraordinary survivors from a bygone era. That, in the harsh economic circumstances in which London Country operated, a crew bus could be found trundling through the wilds of Hertfordshire at 6.45 in the morning was, frankly, remarkable. Even more surprising was the enduring nature of these workings, surviving as they did until May 1976.

The Hertford–Buntingford corridor also featured ANs and RPs during the morning peak, thus adding to the operational variety of the area. Many garages had scheduled RP workings on local bus routes at this time of day, as the last vehicles for Green Line service were not generally required for coach work until well after the peak was over. This continued the former practice (prior to OMO conversion of the Green Line network) whereby RMCs performed odd peak-hour trips.

Some service renumbering occurred in May 1974 in preparation for the introduction of vehicles with three-track number blinds: the 331A became the 337, the 350A became the 351 and the 393A became the 392. Such alterations were very much company policy at the time but in certain cases seemed a little unnecessary; at Hertford, for example, no vehicles equipped with such blinds arrived until November, but in the meantime a complete reissue of RF, RP and RMC destination blinds had to be undertaken.

Further operational variety was provided from August 1974, when the RC class arrived *en masse* from Grays to commence replacement of Hertford's RF fleet. No doubt staff at Hertford were just as enthusiastic about receiving these vehicles as their counterparts at other garages had been in the past. Certainly, had it not been for the progressively worsening vehicle-availability problems apparent throughout the fleet, the chances of their seeing further service — despite their relative youth — would have been slim. They formed the main allocation on routes 327, 331/7, 390 and 392/3, but, in true London Country tradition, there was much inter-working with other services. Narrow (BN-class) Bristol LHSs made their appearance in November, but it was to be the following February before their presence was officially recognised on the schedules; allocation was mainly to routes 308, 333, 386 and 388, but, once again, there was considerable interworking with other services. An interesting reinstatement in May 1975 was that of a service to the villages of Bramfield and Datchworth, abandoned as long ago as August 1971 during the early days of confrontations over subsidies for the rural network, and its restoration demonstrated the far more fruitful relationship now enjoyed between the company and the county councils within its area. Running Tuesdays, Fridays and Saturdays, the new service was numbered 379 and linked Hertford and Stevenage via the aforementioned villages, and, even in the early days of this new venture, passenger numbers were extremely encouraging.

January 1977 saw further restructuring in the Hertford/Hoddesdon area, when routes 310A and 327 were amalgamated into a new 316 operation. Although scheduled for Atlantean operation, the route saw crew-bus substitutions right from the beginning and thus became the very last new service to feature RTs. RT3520 runs through Broxbourne on its way to Enfield on 29 January 1977, the first day of the new service pattern. *Steve Fennell*

Having been the very first Green Line route to receive an RMC allocation in 1962, the 715 survived to become the very last coach route of all to see regular daily operation by these fine vehicles. OMO conversion eventually occurred in April 1972, when the last deliveries of RPs took over, and it seemed thereafter that much of the tradition of Green Line travel had been lost. Just a few weeks before the end, in March 1972, RMC1470 waits outside the now demolished garage at Hertford prior to undertaking the long cross-London trip to Guildford. *Steve Fennell*

The unloved RC class were relegated to bus work in April 1974 and were transferred *en masse* to Hertford, where they replaced a proportion of the garage's RF fleet. They were not well received (hardly unexpected, given their reputation), although the last examples survived until January 1977. Shortly after transfer, RC2 stands at the Nazeing Village terminus of route 327, illustrating the reduced destination display introduced at certain garages in an attempt to increase blind content. *Steve Fennell*

February 1976 witnessed the arrival at Hertford of the Leyland National — the third vehicle type to assist in RF replacement. The garage now operated BNs, RCs, RFs and SNBs on its OMO bus network, although the remaining RFs were replaced by May. Interworkings abounded, with all types seemingly covering all routes. Replaced by Nationals, a number of BNs soon moved on, being required for operation of a new service at Grays. The RCs, meanwhile, reached the end of the road in January 1977, service reductions and further Leyland Nationals providing the means for their replacement. Four examples were retained for training work, although only three would see use in this role. The last survivor, RC10, departed this life in May 1980, having been sold for scrap.

Other alterations that same weekend in January 1977 saw the last remaining crew journeys on route 331 converted to OMO, whilst a new service numbered 316 (Enfield–St Margarets–Hertford) replaced route 310A and partially the 327. Significantly, the 316 was the last new service introduced by London Country to see RT operation, albeit on an unofficial basis. Many garages had retained the odd RT after replacement, whilst several, Hertford included, had re-acquired a member of the type to assist with vehicle shortages, although such operation lasted only until the inevitable CoF expiry. Atlantean availability was often poor, and these odd RTs and even RMCs made regular appearances to help out. An unexpected arrival in July was RML2347, used to prop up the Atlantean allocation on the 310 and 316. This was the first RML to operate from Hertford and was joined in October by three more — RML2354, 2453/5.

Despite the influx of crew buses, November saw the official replacement of all remaining scheduled crew work; three SNBs, released from rural routes by a like number of new BNs, provided the means. However, Hertford's three remaining RMCs — RMC1476, 1500/3 — stayed, so critical was the vehicle situation, and these, together with the aforementioned RMLs, gave an overall total of seven crew buses. Such an abundance of 'goodies' was short-lived, however, as RML2347 suffered CoF expiry in November and RML2453 was returned in November to Staines, where it survived in service until April 1979. Nevertheless, five crew buses remained, and on most days a considerable proportion of the normally AN-operated 310

At London Country's formation, Hertford garage had a scheduled requirement for 27 RFs. Much of this work was predominantly rural in nature, and it came as little surprise when regular reductions occurred as usage decreased. However, while the single-deck fleet had displayed a degree of standardisation in early LCBS days, three different vehicle types were employed to undertake RF replacement: with interworking, most routes ended up served by a mix of RCs, SNBs and BNs. Three months after RF604 was photographed at Broxbourne station on route 392 in May 1974, the 392/393 operation gained the RCs displaced from Grays. All scheduled RF operation at Hertford would cease by February 1976, but the last survivor would not depart until May 1977. *Steve Fennell*

and 316 was covered by these buses. Their collective demise came in April 1978. CoF expiry claimed both the RMLs, while RMC1476 and RMC1503 moved to Garston to help cover for its seriously depleted RML fleet. Despite still having a valid CoF, RMC1500 was transferred to training duties, initially at Stevenage, but it nonetheless managed a few more weeks of stage-carriage service from October 1979, when it was returned to active duty at Northfleet.

Even as late as June 1976 the unexpected could still occur. Having arrived at Hertford to photograph the evening-peak RMC working to Standon on route 331, I was utterly amazed when, completely out of the blue, RT4792 arrived, displaying a full set of RT front blinds. The chase was well and truly on, and this blast from the past was photographed a number of times on its return working to Standon. I also seem to recall getting 'pulled' for speeding in the process — happy days indeed! Here the bus has just passed through Ware *en route* to Standon. *Steve Fennell*

Another surprising working was the use of an RMC to cover the morning peak on routes 350/351 between Hertford and Bishops Stortford. Departing Hertford at 06.37 as a 351, it would return at 07.45 as a 350 from Bishops Stortford. RMC1505 heads away from Ware on the outward 351 working in June 1975.
This particular crew working would be incorporated in the OMO schedule from May 1976. *Steve Fennell*

Other interesting morning-peak workings at Hertford could be found on routes 331 and 337. Each morning an AN would work to Buntingford as a 331, returning to Hertford as a 337, while an RP would run out as a 337, returning as a 331. They were timetabled to occupy the stand at Buntingford at the same time, as demonstrated by AN89 and RP82 in June 1976. *Steve Fennell*

Harlow

THE early days of London Country's operations at Harlow provided considerable interest and variety. Much crew work existed, and an allocation of both RTs and RMLs provided the means for this extensive operation.

The main crew trunk services comprised the 339 (Harlow–Epping–Ongar–Brentwood–Warley) and 397/A (Harlow–Bishops

Although most of Harlow's town services had been converted to OMO in LT days, the odd crew journey survived until August 1979, when crew buses were dispensed with altogether. RT621 leaves Harlow bus station on one such duty in May 1975. *Steve Fennell*

Stortford). The Harlow end of the 397 operation included a 'town' section of route, and in years to come this would be established as a self-standing operation. The 396 (Bishops Stortford–Epping) could also be classed a trunk service but operated only during peak periods.

The town network comprised a series of routes numbered in the 800 series, of which the 804 group (Staple Tye/Harlow Mill–Latton Bush) had received a batch of Autofare MBSs in LT days, although some peak-hour crew workings still survived. Other town services were crew-operated, the 805 (Little Parndon–Potter Street–Epping) and 805A/806 (Little Parndon–Harlow Mill) being the principal operations.

As was the case in other New Towns, the route pattern appeared to be intrinsically complicated, and only the basics are outlined here. Suffice to say such oddities as the 397B, 804B and 805B also existed but in most cases just appeared to be convenient route numbers for a conglomeration of different journeys! In practice, RTs tended to maintain the 339 operation and RMLs the 396/397. However, as was to be expected, considerable interworking occurred, and either type of crew bus could be expected on any service with the exception of route 339, upon which RMLs were at the time considerably rarer. One notable scheduled RML working was on route 393 between Harlow and Broxbourne station. Other crew work comprised the daily allocation on Green Line 718 and a small number of RMCs were maintained for this purpose.

A number of OMO RFs maintained the country operations. Principal routes were the 381 (Harlow–Epping–Toothill/Coopersale) 390 and 393/A, all three of which were shared with Hertford garage. Also RF-operated were the 380 (Bus Station–Mark Hall), which was really more of a town service and might more logically have been numbered in the 800 series, and Green Line 720 (London–Epping–Harlow–Bishops Stortford), plus route 339 on Sundays. In August 1971 the 381 was withdrawn completely as a direct consequence of London Country's policy to withdraw loss-making rural services unless financial support were forthcoming from local authorities. In this case Essex County Council clearly

AN90 was exhibited at the 1972 Commercial Motor Show and was thus afforded the distinction of being delivered in NBC corporate livery. As such it remained unique within the fleet for a number of years, until further repaints became due. Allocated initially to Harlow garage, it is seen at Harlow Mill station on route 811. *Steve Fennell*

Following their arrival at Harlow garage in October 1972, Atlanteans were used mainly on town services. However, the type also operated a handful of peak journeys on routes 396 and 397, upon which normal ticketing methods (as opposed to fareboxes, as on town services) were employed. Displaying an inappropriate 'exact fare' slipboard, AN85 stands at Epping station on an evening peak-hour working. At the time, the 396 operation was split roughly 70:30 in favour of RTs; surprisingly, following service reductions implemented in August 1975, the crew work was retained in preference to the OMO workings. *Steve Fennell*

Having initially lost its RML allocation in October 1972 following the OMO conversion of the town network, Harlow regained the type in January 1977 to replace the hired Southend Leyland PD3s, which themselves had replaced Harlow's last RTs in March 1976. As far as route 397 was concerned, this second phase of RML operation was extremely short-lived, lasting only from January to April 1977, when a restructured pattern of Green Line operations incorporated the vast majority of the service. Still displaying a London Transport radiator badge, RML2351 leaves Harlow bus station on the second 'first day' of RML operation, in January 1977. *Steve Fennell*

declined to assist, although, by way of compensation, a partial replacement service was provided by a local independent operator based in Epping.

February 1972 saw the OMO conversion of route 718 using new RPs. Thanks to the increased running-times such conversions brought, Harlow staff no longer saw Windsor on a regular basis, driver changes now being effected at Staines, whence a Staines driver would undertake the onward return leg to Windsor. Exceptions to this rule were on Bank Holidays, when services to both Hampton Court and Windsor were extremely busy and required considerable duplication. This inevitably produced RMLs and RTs, and normally a high-speed trip could be guaranteed. On such occasions Harlow staff could reacquaint themselves with the canteen facilities at Windsor garage, where a few hours were normally spent before an equally exhilarating return trip!

The first major change to affect operations at Harlow was an extensive scheme implemented in October 1972. As happened the same month at Stevenage, new farebox-fitted ANs were introduced to the entire town network; local journeys on routes 397/A within Harlow were separated to create new services 810/A/811, whilst the MBSs on routes 804/A were also replaced by Atlanteans. The few odd journeys previously

Hired vehicles made their mark at Harlow garage in March 1976, when a batch of Southend Transport Leyland PD3s (previously on hire to London Transport at Croydon) replaced the incumbent RT fleet, which was dispersed for use elsewhere. Undoubtedly impressive vehicles, the PD3s were not well received by the operating staff at Harlow, due, no doubt, to their having manual transmission. Their stay at HA lasted until January 1977, when sufficient Routemasters could be procured from within the fleet to allow their return to Southend. Shortly after introduction, Southend 340 pulls away from Epping station on route 339. *Mike Harris*

operated to Epping under the 805 number became 807s, the original plan to number these as 329s falling by the wayside. A considerable amount of crew operation was lost from this date, but most surprising of all was the despatch of Harlow's entire RML fleet to Staines and Windsor, all remaining crew work now being in the hands of RTs. Some Atlantean journeys were now scheduled on routes 396/397 and the new 807, and these were operated in conventional OMO mode, with the farebox out of use. Crew operation on the remaining town services was very much reduced, but there were still odd RT journeys on the 804 and 806 and journeys were introduced on the 807, 810/A and (later) 811. RT operation now comprised mainly the 339, 396 and 397/A. Also introduced at this time was new express service 812 (Harlow Town Station–Bus Station–Potter Street); this was a two-bus operation worked (somewhat surprisingly) by a pair of SMs.

RPs replaced at Romford by new LNCs arrived in March 1973 to permit the conversion of route 720 from RF operation. However, two RFs remained allocated on Sundays, when the vehicle requirement was greater. At the same time, Sunday operation of route 339 was converted from RF to SM, but in practice the use of Swifts on this service was erratic and normally the allocation remained with the older vehicles. The Sunday RF allocation on the 720 lasted only until May 1974, when the service was extended from Bishops Stortford to Stansted Airport and the Sunday frequency brought into line with that operated on weekdays. RFs still appeared on an unscheduled basis, however, thanks to shortages of RPs. Use of the two SMs to cover RF schedules became commonplace during 1974, thus releasing the RFs for Green Line work; on most days the Swifts could be

found on route 380 or the 392/3 (the 393A having been renumbered 392 in May 1974), the 812 either being operated by Atlanteans or (more likely) suspended due to lack of vehicles.

In 1974 Harlow became the focus for an experiment with 'dial-a-ride' operation, using minibuses. Such vehicles were then very much the exception to the rule and were regarded as a novelty in the few places that they operated. Indeed, in contrast to the situation which would apply a decade or so later, the drivers who manned the service at Harlow received a supplementary allowance on top of their basic wages. Branded 'Pick-Me-Up', it was introduced on 31 August 1974, operated by Ford Transits. Running between the bus station and Old Harlow, the service was sponsored jointly by Harlow District Council, Harlow Development Corporation, Essex County Council and the Department of the Environment's Transport & Road Research Laboratory. At the time it was the biggest such operation to be introduced in Europe. The experiment was to last for two years, and, because of the level of experience to be gained by its operation, any losses were picked up jointly by the sponsors, London Country being merely the agent for its operation. Bookings were taken by telephone at a control office at Harlow bus station, details of booked passengers being passed on by radio to the drivers, who then planned their route accordingly. The service lasted the full two-year period, and much valuable information concerning this type of operation was gathered. In September 1976, following completion of the experimental period, the vehicles were redeployed as a temporary measure on a fixed-route service, again between Old Harlow and the town centre, with an extension to the Princess Alexandra Hospital as required.

A highlight of Bank Holiday operations for many years was the use of RTs and RMLs to work relief journeys on Green Line services. Route 718, serving both Hampton Court and Windsor, was a prime candidate for such duplication, and most Bank Holidays saw two or three Harlow RTs operating throughout to Windsor. A ride on one of these was an exhilarating experience, as a high-speed journey was virtually guaranteed, particularly on the return run to Harlow. RT964 undertakes such a duty on August Bank Holiday Monday in 1974.
Steve Fennell

The first significant changes to the network since the farebox scheme of October 1972 occurred in August 1975. Principal alterations included the conversion of the 380 to farebox AN operation, with the withdrawal of the AN journeys on route 396 and a reduction in AN workings on routes 397/807 as a result. A complete revision of crew schedules also took place, such that the odd RT workings on town routes were completely recast, with journeys now scheduled on the 804, 805, 810A and 811. The newly developed Katherines area of the town was served by a new AN-operated service (808) linking it with the bus station, whilst the 392/393 were diverted via the area *en route* to Hertford and Welwyn.

Five new SNBs were delivered in February 1976, allowing replacement of the last few remaining RFs. In fact, only three RFs were at Harlow prior to the arrival of these buses, the shortfall being made up by the regular use of an SM on an RF working. RF120 was the last example to see service, in March, before moving on to Leatherhead.

At the start of 1976 Harlow was still operating a sizeable number of RTs. The intention had been that from April these would be replaced with RMCs released from Grays following the allocation there of further RCLs displaced by service reductions elsewhere and by OMO conversion of Godstone's 709 route. This would necessarily have been a phased conversion, to be completed by September. Destination blinds had been produced late in 1975 in readiness for the RMCs' arrival, but in the event the conversion did not go ahead as planned, the opportunity having arisen to obtain further hired vehicles. Originally the company had inspected an Ipswich Transport AEC Regent V with a view to hiring a batch for service at Harlow, but this option was not pursued. Instead, 10 Southend Corporation Leyland PD3s were hired, and these entered service from 29 March. Harlow's entire RT stock was dispersed, mostly to Chelsham and Leatherhead, and these PD3s thereafter

covered all scheduled RT workings. One notable exception was the duplication of route 718; as far as Harlow garage was concerned, such work had diminished in recent years, duplication by now occurring only between London and Windsor and covered by Staines garage. However, the duplicate sheet for August Bank Holiday Monday included a crew-operated HA215 booked to work throughout to Windsor. However, the expected Southend PD3 failed to materialise, and in its place arrived AN90, complete with conductor — the first and indeed only time an Atlantean worked the route. By the next Bank Holiday the PD3s would be long gone and the 718 curtailed to operate only between London and Windsor.

RMLs reappeared at Harlow from 29 January 1977, when, following an OMO conversion at Windsor, sufficient vehicles were available to allow the Southend Transport PD3s to return home. Ironically, although some of Harlow's original RMLs had been despatched to Windsor back in 1972, none of these was among the new arrivals. The plan to equip Harlow with RMCs had meanwhile been consigned to history, and the surplus RMCs had instead been allocated to Chelsham, where plans for the OMO conversion of crew work had been deferred. The crew schedule from August 1975 was still in use, and thus the RMLs could be seen covering odd journeys on the town network. However, the Routemasters' return to the 396/397/A was to last only nine weeks, as a major scheme implemented from 2 April would see the conversion of the Harlow–Bishops Stortford corridor to OMO, courtesy of a revised Green Line network: route 718 was withdrawn north of London and the 720 in its entirety, these being replaced by a pair of new services, numbered 702 and 703, running from Bishops Stortford via Harlow and Epping to either Walthamstow Central (702) or Waltham Cross (703). The link provided by route 720 to Stansted Airport was lost, however. Routes 396 and 397A were withdrawn, and the 397 was reduced to just a handful of

The first area within London Country's territory to see minibus operation was Harlow, when a 'Dial-a-Ride' service running under the marketing name of 'Pick-Me-Up' was introduced from August 1974 for a two-year experimental period. Shortly after introduction, FT2 heads for Old Harlow in First Avenue. *Steve Fennell*

OMO peak-hour trips. Other casualties were the limited-stop 812 service and the remnants of the unnumbered former 'Pick-me-up' operation. The requirement for crew buses was thus greatly reduced, and, aside from odd trips on the 807 and 810/A, only the 339 now retained RMLs. However, just three months later, in April, route 339 and all the associated crew workings were converted to OMO using SNBs. Harlow nevertheless retained five RMLs — RML2310/1/50/2/3 — and these saw continued employment on a variety of services. Regular appearances also occurred on the revised Green Line routes 702 and 703, which took the role of limited-stop bus routes. Also introduced in April 1977 was new route 809 (Bus Station–Old Harlow), which replaced the temporary unnumbered minibus operation that had started the previous September following completion of the two-year 'Pick-Me-Up' experiment. The 809 brought to Harlow a small number of BNs, transferred from Leatherhead garage, the latter having received a temporary RF allocation pending delivery of further new BNs.

Of the surviving Routemasters, RML2310/1 were withdrawn in October, and RML2350 moved to Garston in February 1978. Following a schedules revision in May 1978 the remaining pair began operation on a Mon-Sat basis regularly covering workings HA39 and HA40. This move contrived to convert the entire 808 (Sumners–Katherines–Bus Station) service — plus odd workings

on the 804, 805/A and 810/A — to crew operation. August saw the removal of RML2353 to St Albans as a training bus, leaving just RML2352 to maintain a presence on route 808 and, just once in a while, return to the 339. However, due to late deliveries of new Atlanteans, Northfleet garage was experiencing extreme difficulty in maintaining a full service on its remaining crew routes, and a number of unscheduled RMLs were called in from around the fleet to assist. RML2352 thus departed in August 1979 — just over two years since the end of scheduled crew operation at Harlow.

The Harlow area had a considerable number of RPs scheduled for use on bus work during the morning peak, many of these vehicles not being required for Green Line service until later in the morning. RP7 leaves Harlow Mill station on one such working on route 810 in June 1975. *Steve Fennell*

Romford

THE small garage at Romford was unique within the company in operating only Green Line routes. In essence, therefore, it was a 'coach depot' as opposed to a 'bus garage', according to LT/LCBS terminology! Two services were operated — the 721 (London–Brentwood) and 724 (Romford–High Wycombe). The 721 was a long-standing double-deck crew route, RTs having preceded the RCLs delivered in 1965; by contrast, the 724 had been the first Green Line service to feature one-man operation, from its introduction by LT in July 1966.

At London Country's inception the scheduled requirement at Romford was for a mere 18 vehicles. The 721 needed 13 RCLs, with five RFs on route 724 making up the balance. In its day the 721 had been an extremely busy service and even as late as 1970 justified a 12-minute headway at peak times, despite the fact that improved parallel rail services and worsening traffic

Route 724's claim to fame was that, upon introduction in LT days, it was the first Green Line route to be worked by OMO vehicles. By 1972 it had been identified that the resources required to maintain the Rickmansworth–High Wycombe section of route would be better employed by diverting the service via Uxbridge and Heathrow Airport to Staines, thus allowing withdrawal of the costly and regular duplication required on parallel route 727 between Heathrow Airport and St Albans. Romford garage's RF234 is seen at Watford Junction heading for the original western terminus of High Wycombe in March 1970. *Colin Brown*

congestion had contrived gradually to erode its customer base.

The RCLs moved on in January 1972, when, in line with company policy, the 721 became the first service to see its Routemasters replaced by new RPs; the displaced RCLs were transferred to bus work at Reigate and Dorking. RP operation of the 721 was rather short-lived, however, as from February 1973 new Leyland Nationals made their mark. These were LNCs (from the first batch of 11.3m vehicles) and, despite modern external styling, internally represented an appalling alternative to what had gone before — especially the RCLs. Some of the displaced RPs moved across to the 724, while others were transferred to Harlow to permit replacement of RFs. The operations at Romford then commenced a slow, almost painful decline, as regular reductions in frequency combined with ever-increasing traffic problems conspired to cause a continual decline in passenger numbers. The service rapidly descended to the level of a local bus route as remaining long-distance clientèle, put off by worsening traffic conditions and the use of inappropriate vehicles, made alternative travel arrangements.

The writing was, quite literally, on the (garage) wall from April 1977, when the 724, by now operated by Leyland Nationals (albeit to Suburban Coach specification), was transferred to Harlow. The 721, by now requiring just six vehicles, finally ceased on 1 July 1977, Romford garage closing after service that evening.

The 721 was an extremely busy service which linked Aldgate with Romford and Brentwood. In LT days the peak frequency was such that a coach would leave London approximately every six minutes, but, by the time the route passed to London Country, such days had long since passed. Even so, as late as July 1971 the service maintained an advertised 12min peak frequency — still an impressive level of service. OMO conversion came in January 1972, when RPs replaced the well-liked RCLs. There then followed a long period of gradual decline as factors both internal and external took their toll, and the remnants were finally withdrawn in July 1977. In happier days RCL2224 is seen at Romford in July 1971. *Gerald Mead*

The new order on route 721 from February 1973 was the LNC variant of Leyland National. Externally there was no doubt that these were extremely stylish vehicles, but internally they were a terrible comedown from what had only recently passed. Brand-new LNC33 stands at Aldgate Minories bus station in February 1973. *Steve Fennell*

Grays

THE operation at Grays was quite unusual, in that it was almost a separate company within a company. The main link with the rest of the London Country empire was at Romford, where route 370 crossed paths with the 721 and 724. In September 1979 Grays' buses would also reach Brentwood, thanks to a route exchange with Eastern National, but no onward London Country connection would be available, as, from the same date, the section of Harlow's route 339 south of Ongar would be withdrawn and a replacement service provided by... Eastern National! The area thus remained as a self-contained operation and possibly one of the most interesting of the entire London Country network.

Late in LT days Grays had been one of the first garages to receive downgraded Green Line Routemasters, when some workings on routes 370/A (Romford/Purfleet–Tilbury Ferry) gained surplus RMCs. Interworking brought these vehicles onto routes 300 (Stifford Clays–Purfleet), 328B (Purfleet–Ockendon Station) and 371 (Tilbury–Rainham); they also provided the entire

Generally speaking, service revisions saw a reduction in crew-bus operation — particularly odd crew workings on predominantly OMO routes. Just once in a while, however, the unexpected would occur, as was the case with route 323: from April 1976, thanks to some 'spare time' within Grays' crew schedule, a number of off-peak journeys between Grays and Chadwell St Mary (previously single-deck) were converted to Routemaster operation — the first instance of scheduled Routemaster working on this service. RMC1515 is seen within the Alexandra Estate at Chadwell during August 1976. *Steve Fennell*

Sunday allocations on the 300 and 328 (Rainham–Stifford Clays). Grays also possessed an extremely high proportion of crew operation; at London Country's inception the garage's crew-bus allocation totalled 52 vehicles comprising RTs, RMCs and RCLs. By far the most numerous single type was the almost obligatory RT, with 35 examples allocated. Replacement of these vehicles began in January 1972, using Routemasters released by the first OMO conversions of the Green Line network, and so rapid was progress that by April no scheduled RT work remained.

I made a considerable number of visits to Grays during the 'Routemaster period', and such was the operational variety that there was always plenty to see. Although the whole network was extremely localised, the pattern of operation was not heplful to the photographer, who needed to be in two (or even three) places at the same time in order to capture all the action! Nevertheless, the random mixing of RMC/RCL allocations, the many works and peak-hour operations, the odd unscheduled workings and the livery variations contrived to provide endless hours of entertainment. Right at the end of crew operation, in July 1979, I made what turned out to be my last visit to Grays for nigh on 23 years. Only two RMCs remained, and I was surprised to find both of them sitting in the bus station — one on route 328 and the other on the 323. Both were duly photographed, after which, being singularly unimpressed with what else was on offer, I made my escape via the Dartford Tunnel to Gravesend and a further 'fix' of Routemaster operation!

Back to 1972, and in January Grays was one of the first garages to lose its crew Green Line work, when route 723A (London–Rainham–Belhus–Grays–Tilbury) was renumbered 723 and received the peripatetic RCs from Reigate and St Albans. From the same date the original 723, which omitted Belhus, was withdrawn. The RCLs rendered surplus remained at Grays and now formed the main allocation on routes 300, 328, 328A (Stifford Clays–Purfleet) and 328B; interworking brought them to routes 367/368 (Tilbury/Grays–Bata Factory), 369 (Ockendon Station–Aveley), 371A/B (Tilbury–Purfleet/Rainham) and 374 (Linford–Uplands Estate). The entire crew operation was thus well and truly mixed, although a somewhat half-hearted attempt was made to keep the RMCs on the 370/A. Thanks to the unreliability of the RCs, Routemasters maintained a fairly frequent if unpredictable presence on Green Line work; indeed, long after the RCs had gone, this practice continued as vehicle availability plummeted, and the sight of Routemaster coaches fulfilling their traditional role was commonplace for as long as such vehicles remained allocated to Grays.

The RCs moved on yet again in August 1974, this time for use on bus work at Hertford, where a start was made on RF replacement. In their place the 723 received the first examples of the Suburban Coach style of Leyland National delivered to London Country, and these represented a considerable improvement over British Leyland's recent offerings. At last common sense prevailed, with vehicles designed for the medium-to-long-distance market which was Green Line's forte. Had such

The high proportion of crew operation from Grays garage was destined for an early demise as operating costs increased and financial support from Essex County Council declined. Crew work was reduced in February 1973 and again in April 1976, but it was during the summer of 1977 that the axe really fell, cutting the scheduled requirement from 21 in May to two in July. This remnant of operation was itself replaced in January 1979, but a handful of Routemasters remained on an unscheduled basis until CoF expiry curtailed their operation, the last example, RMC1517, being withdrawn in October 1979. Back in May 1975, when the Routemaster was the predominant type in the area, RCL2242 prepares to leave Purfleet Mill Road on route 370A. *Mike Harris*

An unusual purchase was a batch of 15 Bristol VRTs with highbridge Eastern Coach Works bodywork, delivered in June/July 1977. Originally intended for the OMO conversion of route 403 at Chelsham, they were instead sent to Grays to convert the 370 and its associated workings, operating initially as crew vehicles. BT12 is seen at Romford in September 1979. The entire batch would pass to the Bristol Omnibus Co in 1980/1. *Colin Brown*

One of London Country's first tasks was the OMO conversion of most of the remaining crew-operated Green Line routes. January 1972 saw the replacement of RCLs on East London services 721 and 723/A, operated by Romford and Grays garages respectively. RCL2234 is seen at Aldgate Minories bus station on route 723 in September 1971. The majority of Grays' former Green Line fleet remained allocated following conversion, being used to commence replacement of the garage's sizeable allocation of RTs. *Colin Brown*

Belhus Estate plays host to RT3665 on route 328A in July 1971. Again, Routemasters would replace the RT allocation on the 328 group of services during the early part of 1972, but the arrival in February 1973 of a small batch of Atlanteans effectively put paid to the main daytime Routemaster allocation on these services. However, in true Grays fashion, a number of crew workings remained, principally during peak periods. Some route renumbering occurred at the same time, the 328A becoming 329 and the 'B' variation taking the vacant 373 number — all to facilitate the eventual introduction of vehicles with three-track number blinds. *Peter Graves*

standards been adopted back in 1973, when the first Nationals appeared, more of the traditional Green Line network may well have survived.

Further OMO conversions of the Green Line network allowed for more displaced coaches to move in for bus work. Two more RMCs (one each from Harlow and Windsor) arrived in February 1972, followed in March by another four (this time from Stevenage), plus nine RCLs (from Dunton Green). In April an additional seven RMCs rendered surplus at Hertford allowed the completion of RT replacement; in just under five months Grays' entire RT stock had been replaced, and the garage now possessed the company's largest Routemaster allocation.

On the single-deck front, Grays held an RF allocation for routes 323/B (Chadwell St Mary–Purfleet/Uplands Estate), the 371 group and the 374. The 371 group comprised busy services which had been converted from RT to OMO RF only in 1969. AEC Swifts, initially intended by LT for a proportion of RF replacement on busy services, would arguably have been ideal for such routes, but this was destined not to happen under the auspices of London Country.

Given the high proportion of crew work at Grays, it was inevitable that efforts would be made to increase the OMO: crew ratio. February 1973 saw the arrival of a small number of Atlanteans to effect replacement of the allocated RCLs on the 328/A/B; the RCLs moved to route 370, displacing RMCs for transfer to Leatherhead and Reigate, earlier plans for a further Routemaster allocation to Hemel Hempstead being superseded. At the same time, in preparation for the arrival of vehicles with three-track number blinds, the 328A was renumbered 329 and the 328B became 373. Despite the arrival of the Atlanteans, a considerable amount of crew work remained on all three services; renumbering of the 328A/B variations thus necessitated new destination blinds for the Routemasters, but seemingly insufficient were available, as, often as not, the previous numbers continued to be displayed for some months to come.

November 1973 saw an extension to the Atlanteans' sphere of operation when the Sunday workings on routes 300/370/A were so converted. A further seemingly futile service renumbering occurred in February 1974 when the 300 became 375; this was done simply because the 300 number was 'needed' to eliminate 'A'-suffix route 303A at Hatfield, and resulted in yet another reissue of destination blinds. This time the application of the new number was carried out with far more vigour, to the extent that the 375 was 'introduced' almost three weeks prior to the official start date, as I discovered on an expedition to capture some 300s on film! This further change also put paid once and for all to appearances of the aforementioned 328A/B.

New Nationals began replacing the RFs on routes 323/371/A/B in February 1976, this allocation being formalised the following month. Just one RF remained on a scheduled basis, for route 374, and this survived for only a few weeks pending the arrival of a small number of BNs. The primary function of these vehicles was to open up new areas of the town to a bus service, physical restrictions precluding larger vehicles; the 374 also required a small vehicle to negotiate the turning-point at East Tilbury Village and was the only London Country route to undertake a reversing manœuvre with passengers aboard.

Despite the changes, Grays still possessed a disproportionately high level of scheduled crew work. Essex County Council had long been making noises over the level of subsidy required to maintain the existing network, and it was thus only a matter of time before the effects of such discussions would be felt. The first wave of changes occurred in April 1976, when some long-standing route numbers disappeared and reductions and restructuring effectively removed six crew buses from the schedules. Interworking was still rife, however, and crew buses and OMO Atlanteans were now scheduled on certain journeys on the 323 and new route 324 (Chadwell St Mary–Purfleet). The displaced RMCs made their way to Chelsham and Leatherhead; Grays had long been a 'buffer zone' for crew

Despite the aforementioned OMO conversion of the 371 group in 1969, a considerable number of crew workings remained at Grays, whose RT1009 is seen covering a peak-hour working on the 371B variant in July 1971. The garage's entire RT fleet would be replaced during the first few months of 1972 as Routemaster coaches displaced from Green Line service arrived for bus work, ensuring that crew operation would continue for some time. *Peter Graves*

buses, much as Crawley was for the OMO fleet, and RMCs and RCLs were frequently swapped according to vehicle requirements throughout the fleet. Reductions elsewhere now threw up spare RCLs, and these were used to release RMCs for transfer elsewhere, either for replacement of the few remaining RTs or to cover shortages.

May 1977 saw another round of swingeing service reductions, which ultimately allowed for a further decrease of crew bus requirements. The scheduled number of remaining RCLs was now down to 13. All RMC work officially ceased, and surplus vehicles moved to Leatherhead and Reigate to advance the conversion of route 406 from RT. Remaining crew work was now primarily on the 370, with odd trips (in some cases just single journeys) remaining on the 323, 328, 367, 371, 373 and 374. Further hefty reductions also occurred at the same time, resulting in a significant decrease in peak-hour activity on the Grays–Purfleet corridor. A considerable number of spare RCLs nevertheless remained to cover for non-existent OMO buses, but this was very much a short-term option, as, from the following month, new Bristol VRs — the BT class — entered service as crew buses. The RCLs thus displaced were used on the special Epsom Downs service in connection with the annual Derby sweepstakes, before settling primarily at Chelsham.

Yet more upheavals occurred from July, when the newly introduced BTs lost their conductors, the 370 becoming an OMO operation. From the same date the Atlanteans moved on, replaced by the BTs and a handful of new Leyland Nationals. From an allocation of 21 crew buses in May, the requirement had now fallen to two, with workings on routes 323 and 328. However, as was to be expected in such circumstances, some additional RCLs remained on an unscheduled basis, and these, coupled with the inevitable surfeit of conductors, provided a sensible medium-term solution in the absence of sufficient new vehicles. Indeed, unscheduled crew operation remained a regular feature at Grays for some time.

The number of crew buses at Grays fluctuated considerably over the next couple of years, even though the scheduled requirement never exceeded two. Immediately following the July 1977 cull, six RCLs remained, but by October 1978 all had either moved on to more worthy causes or had suffered CoF expiry. Surprisingly, seven Routemasters (five RCLs and two RMCs) were procured from around the fleet and transferred in to maintain a similar level of crew-bus cover. Some worked for only a few weeks, however, and only three RCLs and the RMCs survived into 1979. The small amount of remaining crew work was officially converted to OMO in January 1979 to coincide with CoF expiry of the surviving RCLs. RCL2250 was the last of its class to operate in service for London Country, retaining its traditional Lincoln green to the end; its last day in service is believed to have been 24 January.

The last two operational RMCs at Grays were RMC1475 and RMC1517, both of which arrived in March 1979 to replace CoF-expired examples. The final few months' operation of these two survivors still saw a remarkable daily variation in services operated, but the highlight was undoubtedly their use on a semi-regular basis on working GY80, which covered a morning peak journey on route 723 between Grays and East Ham. Obviously whoever at Grays was responsible for their daily allocation still had a deep-rooted sense of tradition. RMC1475 suffered CoF expiry in August, and it thus fell to RMC1517, which followed suit in October, to bring down the curtain on what had once been one of the most comprehensive areas of crew operation in the London Country empire.

The conversion of the busy 371 group from RT to OMO RF in October 1969 was the last major scheme undertaken by London Transport prior to the formation of London Country Bus Services as a subsidiary of the National Bus Company. RF687 is seen in Grays town centre on the 371 during April 1973. At this time, RF operation at Grays still had almost three years left to run, Leyland Nationals eventually providing the means of replacement from February 1976. *Steve Fennell*

Northfleet

ACROSS the river from Grays, Gravesend was served by both London Country — from its Northfleet garage — and Maidstone & District.

Northfleet garage was another whose operations included a high proportion of crew work; routes 480 (Erith–Dartford–Gravesend–Denton), 487 (Swanscombe–Gravesend Singlewell/Kings Farm) and 498 (Gravesend–Painters Ash–Northfleet) were all RML-operated. Routes 495 and 496 (Northfleet–Kings Farm Estate) had been converted to OMO in LT days using Autofare MBSs, whilst a sizeable RF fleet was also maintained, primarily for Green Line work and the surviving rural operations on the Gravesend–Ash/New Ash Green corridor. The rural operations had seen considerable pruning early on in London Country days, and routes 451 (Gravesend–Betsham–Hartley Court), 452 (Dartford–Longfield–West Kingsdown) and 489/A (Gravesend–Longfield–Ash/Meopham) had all ceased by January 1972. The surviving network was restructured to cover some of the missing links and metamorphosised into two basic services, the 450 (Dartford–Bean–Gravesend) and 490/A (Gravesend–Hartley Court/Ash). Further reductions in July 1973 saw Hartley Court lose its service; the 490A was renumbered 489 and provided the main link between Gravesend–Longfield and Ash, whilst the 490 became a Gravesend–Longfield–New Ash Green operation. Prior to this, in March 1972, the new SMA class had arrived at Northfleet, displacing RFs from route 725 (Gravesend–Croydon–Kingston–Windsor); the route's Dartford and Windsor allocations were similarly replaced at this time.

One aspect of the Gravesend area was the reincarnation of former route numbers, in many cases to almost exact past areas of operation, when service alterations occurred. In July 1973 there were two such instances, one of which was the 489 described above; the other saw the return of the 488 in an attempt to simplify the intricacies of the extremely complicated 487 network. RML-operated, this used three different termini at Swanscombe, whilst at its other extremity it served either the Singlewell area or Kings Farm Estate. In LT days part of this convolution had used the number 488, and this reappeared as part of the restructuring. The Swanscombe area saw the introduction of a loop working to replace the varied selection of termini. Journeys to Singlewell retained the 487 number, whilst those to Kings Farm took up the vacant 488. In the best London Country tradition, some anomalies over termini still occurred, particularly at weekends, but the revisions represented a considerable simplification of what had gone before.

The RF allocation was replaced both on local bus and Green Line work in September 1974. The 701 (Gravesend–London–Ascot) received new SNCs of the Suburban Coach variety, so those who used the service never had to endure the niceties of a bus-seated National. (Unknown at the time was that the 701 had only a further 13 months to live and would be withdrawn without replacement at very short notice in October 1975.) Later that September, the first of the narrower BN version of the Bristol LHS entered service on the 450/489/490 group. Originally it was thought that BLs would provide the necessary replacement; unfortunately physical restrictions precluded their introduction, but, in a rare stroke of fortune, training had already been undertaken using the wider vehicles, and consequently the majority of operating staff had already obtained their (manual) licences. Thus little time was wasted between the delivery of the BNs and their entry into service. However, this was not quite the end of RFs at Northfleet, as random allocations continued throughout the ensuing years.

Further tinkering with the crew-bus network occurred in August 1975. One of the features was the introduction of a 482 route, which shared common ground with route 480 between

Northfleet's RMLs, the final operation of which encompassed route 480, were amongst the last of the type to operate within the company, with conversion to Atlantean (initially crew-operated) commencing in November 1979. Towards the end of their lives these Routemasters presented an appalling external appearance, attributable in part to the cement dust-laden atmosphere of the area and also, sorry to say, a certain amount of 'in-house' neglect. During the last summer of operation, RML2325, in typical external condition for the time, approaches the Valley Drive terminus at Gravesend. Valley Drive itself was relatively new territory for London Country, the 480 having been extended into this former Maidstone & District stronghold only in October 1976. *Steve Fennell*

A particularly well-travelled Routemaster was RMC1490. Following the application of an overall advertisement livery for London & Manchester Assurance in March 1973, it embarked on a 'tour' encompassing Grays, Reigate, Northfleet, Windsor, High Wycombe and Garston garages, normally spending about eight weeks at each. During July 1975 a revised London & Manchester livery was applied, after which the bus continued its nomadic existence before finally reverting to fleet livery in April 1977. Displaying the original L&M scheme, it is seen at Hever Court Estate, Gravesend, on 18 August 1974, during its second visit to the area. *Mike Harris*

In January 1972 the company received the first of a batch of Alexander-bodied AEC Swifts destined originally for South Wales Transport. Thanks to a fairly early decision to divert these vehicles, they benefited from the inclusion of a number of defining LT-style features, standard single-deck destination displays and the style of seat moquette carried by contemporary LT and LCBS deliveries being the two most noticeable. The majority were destined to spend virtually their entire working lives on the south-orbital 725 route (and the later 726 variation), upon which SMA4, in later NBC corporate colours, is seen at Hampton Court in August 1978. *Geoff Rixon*

The acquisition of the relatively small fleet of Bristol LHSs could be attributed to the need for a further source of vehicles to allow replacement of elderly LT-designed types as well as for a type suitable for routes where physical restrictions (perceived or otherwise) applied. Their non-standard nature, coupled with manual transmission, did not exactly endear them to those involved in their daily operation, and most were fated for short working lives with London Country, especially after it was 'discovered' that many of the routes served by these vehicles could accommodate 10.3m Leyland Nationals. Brand-new BN61 stands outside Dartford garage whilst working from Northfleet on route 450 in May 1978. *Colin Brown*

Erith and Gravesend and then took over the Singlewell leg of the 487. The 487 took over the Kings Farm leg of the 488, whilst the 488 itself was re-routed to Denton, the long-standing terminus of route 480. The 498 operations remained unchanged. Surprisingly the Sunday workings — other than the 498, which had succumbed to OMO RF operation in July 1973 and been converted to BN the following September — remained crew-operated

A rather more radical programme of service revisions occurred in October 1976, when an exchange of work took place between London Country and Maidstone & District. The 480 was extended from Denton to Valley Drive, replacing the M&D 306, whilst the 487/488 operations were revised to cover M&D's 305, thus linking both Singlewell and Kings Farm in a large loop that also served the Valley Drive area. The recently introduced 482 was dispensed with, as was the 498, which was covered by an extension of M&D's 307/308; the evening and Sunday bifurcations, which took 498s to Singlewell and Kings Farm, were absorbed in the revised 487/488 service, which also saw conversion to OMO on Sundays. Significantly, all the M&D services had been OMO, whereas their London Country replacements (initially, at least) were all crew-operated.

OMO conversion of Monday-Saturday operation of the 487/488 was to have begun in May 1977 using MBS vehicles, but insufficient were available, and RMLs continued to cover throughout the summer on a 50:50 basis. 'Plan B' allowed for the procurement of further MBSs in July, but this failed to happen, and it was not until October that sufficient of the class were available to allow the full conversion.

The closure of the Maidstone & District garage in Gravesend, on the last day of March 1978, allowed for transfer of M&D's 307 and 308 routes to London Country from 1 April. The Gravesend–Northfleet leg of these two routes had been transferred to M&D only in October 1976 (in exchange for the Valley Drive extensions applied to the 480/487/488). London Country now renumbered them as 497 and 498, the latter number making a comeback to its former territory. The Leyland National made its reappearance at Northfleet (the earlier batch having already departed, following withdrawal of route 701) with the SNBs introduced for these new services, but insufficient were available initially, and a partial MBS allocation was retained for the first three months. Also from 1 April the Sunday operation of route 480 was converted to OMO using the aforementioned SNBs, whilst BNs maintained the Sunday workings on the 497/498.

Many former London Transport vehicles throughout the fleet met their demise in 1979, and to all intents and purposes the year was the turning-point after which London Country became 'just another NBC operator'. Small pockets of LT influence remained at various locations as the year dawned, but further deliveries of Nationals and Atlanteans soon put paid to such traditions. Northfleet was no exception to this policy, and by the year's end only a handful of Merlins and Routemasters remained. Further SNBs arrived in July, replacing the MBSs on the 487/488, whilst the Merlins on the 495/496 were progressively replaced throughout December. Three MBSs survived into 1980 but saw little use, and all were withdrawn in March. Northfleet's final RF 'died' in July 1979, following gearbox failure. The bus concerned, RF202, had been a surprising survivor,

along with RF221. Both had been recertified at Northfleet in June 1977; RF221 had then moved immediately to Dartford, but RF202 had remained fairly active at Northfleet, participating mainly in local bus operation but also making the occasional sortie onto Green Line work. It was resurrected for the Green Line Golden Jubilee celebrations in 1980 and remained thereafter as an official company-preserved vehicle.

The Routemaster situation deteriorated rapidly from April 1979. CoF expiry was taking its toll and the planned replacement Atlanteans were still to be delivered. RMLs were purloined from throughout the fleet, in the process ending all the unscheduled operations elsewhere, but still insufficient were available. Such was the situation that two examples were returned to service from training duties, and many workings were covered by crew-operated single-deckers. All manner of different vehicle types appeared on the 480 that last summer, including BNs, SMAs and even MBSs — all carrying conductors. Relief was at hand from November as the first new Atlanteans made their presence felt, and most of the single-deck variation finished soon after. Once delivery finally commenced, the flow of Atlanteans was extremely rapid, and by the year's end only two RMLs remained; a handful moved elsewhere to eke out their final days, but the vast majority suffered CoF expiry. RML2446, destined to be the last of its type in service at Northfleet, managed to operate on route 496 on 6 December, and this and one other example survived into 1980. The last day of RML operation, on the 480, is believed to have been 16 February 1980, when RML2446 covered working NF13. The route dispensed with the use of conductors in April 1980, when possibly the company's busiest route was converted to OMO.

Northfleet's last scheduled RFs were those allocated to routes 450, 489 and 490, and these were replaced by Bristol LHSs in September 1974. Similarly converted at the same time was the Sunday OMO working of route 498; RF48 represents the old order in Gravesend town centre during the summer of 1974. A modernised RF, it carries overall NBC leaf green without any form of relief — a style applied locally at Northfleet garage as repaints became due. One should perhaps be thankful that only three such vehicles were afforded this treatment! Steve Fennell

Dartford

Despite receiving newer vehicles in the form of SMA-class Alexander-bodied Swifts early in 1972, route 725 still saw plenty of RF activity. RF596, a standard bus example operating from Dartford garage, is seen at Windsor in August 1975. *Steve Fennell*

THE principal OMO conversions which occurred throughout the southeast area of the LCBS domain in July 1971 were far-reaching, and, in the case of Dartford garage, saw new SMs replace RTs on the majority of workings on the 401 (Belvedere–Dartford–Sevenoaks), 401A (Belvedere–Joydens Wood), 423 (Longfield–Dartford– Swanley–Wrotham), 467 (Sidcup–Dartford–Horton Kirby) and 491 (Belvedere–Dartford–Horton Kirby). Of these services, the 401/A and 423 were shared with Swanley. Inevitably, interworking also brought Swifts to other routes, and crew operation at Dartford was reduced to just the 499 (Downs Estate–Joyce Green Hospital). Again, in true London Country fashion, interworking brought crew buses to some predominantly OMO services.

Dartford's final few RTs moved on in February 1972 with the arrival of RMCs rendered redundant at Harlow and Windsor. These took over the operation of route 499 and odd journeys on the 401, 423 and 480. The 480 was notable in that Dartford operated only a tiny proportion of this service — primarily a handful of early-morning Monday–Friday journeys. Other crew trips included odd journeys on route 423A between Watchgate, Joyce Green and the Wells firework factory on Dartford Marshes, the 423B to Littlebook power station and the 423C to Downs School. All these services featured just a small number of journeys a day — primarily during the peaks and at school times — and operation was shared on an almost equal basis with OMO types. Even more notable, however, was the allocation of crew buses on Sundays. Away from their regular 499, RMCs operated short-working journeys on route 401 between Dartford and Bexleyheath and on the 423 between Dartford and Watchgate; such operation was inevitably due to scheduling constraints — spare time existed within the crew schedule but insufficient within the OMO roster to allow driver-only operation of these trips. Suffice to say they were surprisingly

resilient, and it was not until August 1975 that the entire Sunday operation, 499 included, dispensed with conductors.

Notwithstanding the mass Swift invasion in 1971, Dartford possessed a reasonable proportion of RF work on both bus and Green Line services. Route 486 (Dartford–Belvedere) had been converted from RT to RF fairly late in LT days; the 725 also featured RFs but only until March 1972, when Dartford received a share of the new SMA class to provide replacement. Such were the intricacies of interworkings that a morning-peak journey on the 423B was also operated by one of these SMAs! Unfortunately neither these nor the mechanically similar SMs were particularly reliable, and a feature of operations at most garages blessed with either type was the retention of additional RFs to provide cover. Dartford was no exception, and, despite the planned conversion of the 486 to SM from summer 1975, an RF presence was still maintained until September 1978. One particularly interesting scheduled RF working was that of a return trip, late on Saturday evenings, from Dartford to Erith on route 480!

The effects of vehicle shortages took a totally unexpected twist towards the end of 1975, when London Country commendably took the initiative and hired buses from other companies to maintain services. Dartford garage drew the short straw when, in November, its RMCs were transferred *en bloc* to Garston and replaced with a batch of Maidstone Corporation Leyland PD2As. Leyland devotees will doubtless disagree, but, compared with the refined nature of an RMC, these PD2s were appalling contraptions. They were sluggish and draughty, and their internal specification bore no comparison. A definite minus-point in the eyes of drivers used to semi-automatic transmission was the fact that they possessed a gearstick and a clutch; given the hilly terrain of the area, some interesting driving techniques emerged! The climb from Dartford into the Temple Hill Estate was a case

in point: most drivers would take a run at the hill in the hope of making the first stopping-point without having to change down; others, having persuaded the gearbox to accept second, would simply leave the vehicle in that gear and plod up the hill, engine screaming. I spent an interesting hour one afternoon at this point filming these buses, and my lasting regret is that I didn't have a microphone on the camera to record the sound-effects, which were quite entertaining! By September 1976 the vehicle situation had eased sufficiently to allow for the RMCs to return and the PD2s were despatched back to Maidstone, bringing to a close an interesting period of London Country history. Few tears were shed at their departure, but one cannot deny that these vehicles served an extremely useful purpose during one of the worst periods of vehicle availability.

The return of Dartford's Routemaster fleet was to be short-lived, as from July 1977 the remaining crew work was converted to OMO using further SMs. All bar one of the RMCs were transferred away, most to Chelsham; the survivor — RMC1457 — was unserviceable anyway. Surprise arrivals just prior to conversion were a couple of RCLs. Displaced from Grays in June, these were *en route* to Chelsham, which they eventually

reached in July; during the interim they were employed alongside the incumbent RMCs. August saw the return of two of Dartford's original RMCs — RMC1459/62 — whilst RMC1457 was relicensed in September. These three vehicles were used on an *ad hoc* basis, covering for the inevitable Swift shortfall, and saw operation on a number of services until December, when two of them suffered CoF expiry; RMC1457 survived as the last of its breed at Dartford before finally moving on to Chelsham in March 1978.

Leyland Nationals had been a familiar sight in the town since July 1977, when an initial allocation had been made to Swanley. Swifts displaced from Swanley had enabled the conversion of the 499 to OMO, it apparently not being an option to allocate new Nationals to Dartford at that stage. It was therefore not until December 1978 that three Nationals arrived at Dartford, ostensibly to begin replacing the large SM fleet now operated. In reality, for the first few weeks, they were used to cover for CoF-expired SMAs on Green Line work, due to the late delivery of new Duple-bodied Reliances earmarked for route 725. The initial trio were joined in June 1979 by another eight examples, and further deliveries ensured that by December only one scheduled SM remained, although six were retained for spare cover. By September 1980 this total had been whittled down to just three — SM469, 514/7; quite amazingly, SM514/7 still retained the traditional livery of Lincoln green — the last vehicles within the fleet to do so. These three SMs managed to cling on for a few more weeks, being finally withdrawn on receipt of replacement SNBs late in November 1980.

Swanley

SWANLEY garage also participated in the July 1971 OMO conversions which affected this part of the London Country empire. Its relatively small RT fleet survived just a little longer than that at Dartford, the 477 and associated odd workings being converted to RMC in April 1972. Originally Swanley's remaining RT operations had been intended to receive RCLs, with the RMCs going instead to Crawley and Reigate for the 405/B (leading, presumably, to a mixed RMC/RCL operation at either Crawley or Reigate); in the event, due to concerns expressed by the operating staff over physical restrictions, RMCs were allocated as a compromise, an agreement having been reached that buses would not be scheduled to pass on certain sections of route. Aside from the main operation on the 477, crew buses made sorties on the 401A, 423, 423A and also the evening service on the 493 (Orpington–Ramsden Estate). The 401A and 423A operations were both short-lived, but the 423 retained some crew journeys until April 1978, whilst the 493 retained RMC workings right up until the type's replacement in 1980. One highlight of the 423 was the use (until August 1975) of an RMC throughout the evening peak on a Dartford Heath–Longfield–Wrotham–Swanley circuit; conversely, certain evening-peak workings on the 477 were booked for SMs. The 493 operation demonstrated another interesting variation so often favoured by London Country: the main daytime service was operated by Dunton Green garage with OMO single-deck vehicles, but it was more economic for the evening service to work off route 477, as sufficient 'slack' existed within the schedule. Thus, to photograph a 493 RMC one had to make the effort in June, as the first trip was at approximately 20.30hrs. Fortunately a Sunday-afternoon service was introduced with the same method of operation in August 1975, which made life a lot easier.

January 1974 saw the arrival of the garage's first Leyland

Nationals, for RF replacement on route 719 (Wrotham–London–Hemel Hempstead). Swanley was one of the few garages that had no scheduled RF bus operation, but such was the availability of the resident SM fleet that the presence of unscheduled RFs was essential if any semblance of a full vehicle run-out was to occur. By 1976 CoF expiry had put paid to the vast majority of rogue RF allocations around the fleet, and the last serviceable example departed from Swanley that summer.

Hired vehicles made their mark at Swanley in January 1976, when three AEC Regent Vs from Eastbourne Corporation displaced a like number of RMCs to help out at Northfleet, which was experiencing the usual problems with RML availability. During the 1970s the loan of Swanley's RMCs to Northfleet was a fairly regular (but unpredictable) occurrence as the latter garage struggled to maintain sufficient crew buses for service. The Regent Vs were impressive vehicles and did not appear to have the 'acceptance' problems that the PD2s encountered at Dartford; although they stayed only six months (being returned to Eastbourne in June), they seemed popular amongst the operating staff and regularly saw service on Sundays, even though sufficient RMCs were available.

Crew bus shortages arising during 1977 were dealt with 'in house'; for a few weeks during June/July, two RCLs displaced from Grays were gainfully employed and, despite the objections to their use that had been raised in 1972, appeared to operate without difficulty.

New SNBs intended for SM replacement arrived in July 1977. Redundant Swifts moved to Dartford to eliminate remaining crew work, whilst others were used to provide cover for the overhaul/recertification programme. Insufficient new SNBs were available initially to replace the entire allocation, and four Swifts remained. It was intended that these four remaining

As a further means of alleviating vehicle shortages, three hired Eastbourne Corporation AEC Regent Vs entered service at Swanley garage from January 1976. These buses seemingly had none of the 'acceptance' problems that bedevilled various other hired offerings, and they settled down to give a good account of themselves until the hire ceased in June the same year. Allocated to route 477, they saw regular seven-days-a-week operation, even though sufficient quantities of the more usual RMCs were available on Sundays. Eastbourne 68 is seen at Swanley Junction in April 1976. *Mike Harris*

Despite OMO conversion of route 423 in July 1971, some journeys, operated by both Dartford and Swanley garages, retained crew operation. Undoubtedly the highlight of these workings was the evening-peak operation, when an RMC traversed the entire route from Longfield to Wrotham. Inevitably such crew forays were doomed, and OMO conversion of this and most other odd workings on this service occurred from August 1975. In June 1974, a tidy-looking RMC1514, still in Lincoln green, passes through Swanley *en route* to Wrotham. *Colin Stannard*

RMCs arrived at Swanley in April 1972 to replace the garage's last RTs, employed on route 477. The longer RCL variant had been the original choice, but physical restrictions in the Crockenhill area precluded the type's use. The RMCs would be a regular sight for almost eight years, and the 477 would have the honour of providing the last regular crew operation within the company, albeit using new Atlanteans for its final 12 months. It would nevertheless play host to London Country's very last Routemaster operation, the last rites being performed on 5 March 1980 by RMC1512. Some years earlier, in June 1976, RMC1465 arrives at Dartford displaying a localised 'via' blind for short workings between Dartford and Wilmington. *Steve Fennell*

examples would be replaced in October, but vehicle shortages still precluded this; a 'paper' conversion still occurred, but it was not until March 1978 that the last serviceable example, SM101, was transferred out. This was not quite the end of SM operation from Swanley, however, as a number of vehicles remained allocated to Dartford as spare vehicle cover, ostensibly for both garages. SMs were thus loaned on a day-to-day basis, and this practice continued into the summer of 1980.

Further revisions occurred in April 1978, including the withdrawal of the London–Wrotham leg of the 719. Maidstone & District route 919 provided part replacement, whilst a peak-hour Green Line facility was provided from Borough Green to London, numbered 729; race days at Brands Hatch were catered for by a 739 variation. Considerable reductions were made to local bus services from the same date, notable among which was the curtailment of the long-standing 401 route at Eynsford. The section thence to Sevenoaks was withdrawn without replacement, apart from a sparse (and short-lived) Sunday operation, the purpose of which was to maintain the through link to the Dartford hospitals. The West Kingsdown–Wrotham section of the 423 also suffered the same fate, as did the few remaining crew journeys on the same service.

Swanley's main claim to fame in the late 1970s was as home to the company's last Routemaster operation. By the summer of 1979 six RMCs remained, and these continued to see not only daily service on the 477 but also the evening and Sunday workings on the 493. Surprising was the fact that conductors were still rostered on Sundays and indeed remained so, even after conversion of the route to Atlantean operation. The initial plan was that all surviving Routemasters would be withdrawn by the year's end, but delivery of the replacement Atlanteans was delayed, and traditional crew operation survived into 1980. The first Atlantean did not arrive at Swanley until November 1979, its first day in service, following type training, being 17 December. Further examples arrived as the month progressed, but not in sufficient numbers to provide a complete allocation. RMC availability was poor, but, as the New Year dawned, four remained available for service. One surprise was the arrival in January of RML2445, but its use was spasmodic; no doubt its open platform and lack of saloon heaters had some bearing on this, and it moved on to Chelsham later in the month. The official date set for full Atlantean conversion was 16 February 1980, but in practice a full AN allocation was available throughout the preceding week. One RMC still remained licensed, however, and this lone example, RMC1512, continued to make random appearances in service throughout the month. London Country commendably organised a 'Routemaster Farewell Tour' for Saturday 1 March, although somewhat embarrassingly the special destination blinds provided mis-spelled Routemaster as 'Routmaster'. Two buses — the aforementioned RMC1512 and Northfleet's RML2446 — were provided and extensively toured former Routemaster haunts of the South East area. This was fully intended to be the last duty for the surviving Routemasters and indeed was advertised as such, but, despite such proclamations, vehicle availability dictated RMC1512's reappearance on stage service, and it operated for two further days — 4/5 March — on route 477. This really was the end, however, and it was pleasing that the last operation epitomised a normal day's service undertaken by the rostered crew, in much the same way as had occurred on a daily basis since the introduction of Routemasters to the 477 in April 1972.

A major OMO conversion befell operations at Dartford and Swanley garages in July 1971, when new SMs replaced the bulk of RT operations on routes 401/A, the 423 group and the 467/491. Despite the influx of OMO vehicles, some crew workings remained, including a somewhat curious (and doubtless uneconomic) Sunday operation from Dartford encompassing some afternoon and evening trips on routes 401 and 423. RTs were initially retained for this relatively small remnant of crew operation, but during March and April 1972 displaced Routemaster coaches arrived to consign regular RT operation in this part of the London Country empire to history. Back in June 1971, however, the green RT was still a common sight in the area, as exemplified at Dartford by RT3422 on route 401 and RT4047 on the 477, destined to be London Country's very last crew route. *(upper) Tom Maddocks, (lower) Ken Harris*

Dunton Green

DUNTON Green garage was one of the first to lose the LT influence completely, having the dubious honour of being the first to receive a production batch of Leyland Nationals for normal bus operation and sharing with St Albans the distinction of receiving the first examples of the Bristol LHS. It was also a participant in the major crew-to-OMO conversion of July 1971, featuring the LT-ordered Swifts. The removal of all its crew work was effected very rapidly, and by March 1972 the garage was able to boast a full OMO allocation on all services. Such was the state of vehicle availability that crew operation would return in October 1975, but, yet again, in circumstances that could not have been imagined earlier in the decade.

The July 1971 programme saw new Swifts replace the RTs on the Croydon–Sevenoaks–Tonbridge corridor, which received the 403A route number; the new vehicles also worked odd journeys on the 402 (Bromley–Sevenoaks–Tonbridge) and 454/A (Chipstead– Sevenoaks–Tonbridge). Crew work remaining at this time comprised the 421/A (Sevenoaks–Heverham) and the majority of the aforementioned 454/A, plus the Green Line operations on the 704/5 (Tunbridge Wells/Sevenoaks–London–Windsor).

The outstanding crew-bus work ceased early in 1972; a combination of further Swifts and a handful of RFs put paid to the few remaining RTs in January, while, just two months later, new RPs displaced the RCLs from the 704/705. In true Country Bus tradition, the RCLs had operated some journeys on local bus routes prior to taking up normal Green Line work. Notable was a double-deck working on route 431A (Sevenoaks–Green Street Green–Orpington); the same vehicle would subsequently undertake a trip on the 493 (Chelsfield–Orpington Ramsden Estate). Upon OMO conversion these journeys ceased, but RPs would eventually appear on the vast majority of

Dunton Green's bus services as availability of new-generation OMO vehicle types plummeted.

New Year's Day 1973 saw the arrival of a small batch of Leyland Nationals intended for RF replacement on route 493. These were the first examples of the production batch intended for normal bus work and represented very much the 'shape of things to come' throughout the company. They also operated odd journeys on routes 431/471 (Sevenoaks–Chelsfield/Cudham–Orpington) and appeared slightly incongruous alongside the RFs which normally worked these predominantly rural services. Further RF replacement occurred in October, when a small batch of BL-class Bristol LHSs commenced operation on route 404 (Shoreham–Sevenoaks– Ide Hill), with inevitable interworkings on other services.

Aside from a fleeting visit just before the 704/705 conversion in March 1972, when the option of an illicit Green Rover expedition was considered preferable to a day at school, my first camera-equipped foray to the area was coincidentally on the first day of BL operation. Inevitably curiosity got the better of me, and a round trip to Ide Hill was undertaken on one of the new buses. It was not a pleasant experience: the ride quality was appalling, and, although the driver had undoubtedly mastered the manual transmission, the seeming lack of suspension provided some 'interesting' moments! Interior noise levels were also quite high, and the whole journey was in complete contrast to the quiet and smooth-running RF I encountered when making my escape from the area. Fortunately London Country never had much enthusiasm for the LHS, and most had a relatively short life-span within the company. Inevitably some garages occasionally employed them as spares on Green Line work, and, to be fair, their ride quality on relatively well-maintained main roads was infinitely superior to that on pot-holed country lanes. However, although they provided some operational variety, they were generally an extremely poor substitute for what had gone before.

March 1975 saw the arrival of some SNBs to commence replacement of the garage's remaining stock of RFs. On paper, at least, Dunton Green's last RFs were replaced in May 1976 by further Swifts, but three examples lingered on. RF103 and RF129 suffered CoF expiry in

Dunton Green's last RTs were replaced in January 1972, leaving only the Green Line operations on routes 704 and 705 to retain conductors for a few months. The last scheduled RT work was on routes 421/A and 454/A; in this undated photograph (thought to have been taken during summer 1971) RT4495 arrives at Sevenoaks on the afternoon peak 421A journey from Kemsing. *Steve Fennell collection (photographer unknown)*

Brand-new RP71, allocated to Dunton Green garage, passes through Hammersmith on route 704. Finished in traditional Green Line attire, these stylish vehicles appeared well capable of upholding the standards that had for so long been part of Green Line tradition. Unfortunately a series of various deficiencies, both mechanical and otherwise (non-operable saloon heating being the most noticeable from a passenger viewpoint), soon caused a fall from favour, and many had short working lives with London Country. *Colin Brown*

July, ostensibly leaving just RF236 to run for a few more months until the inevitable CoF expiry would necessitate its demise. However, in traditional London Country manner, RF242 was transferred in from Chelsham in July to spend the remainder of the year substituting for newer vehicle types, and, like RF236, seemed to spend most of its time covering for RPs on Green Line work. (A number of garages had uneasy relationships with their RPs, and Dunton Green was no exception: quite often, whilst the RFs were plying their trade on Green Line work, the displaced RPs would find themselves being used on local bus services, whence it was considerably easier to recover them in the event of a failure.) Both surviving RFs suffered CoF expiry at the end of the year, and with them went another small remnant of the LT legacy.

Such shortages contrived to return crew operation to Dunton Green in October 1975. In a highly significant move, six former Royal Blue Bristol MWs were hired to replace Swifts, mainly on routes 413 (Sevenoaks–Chipstead) and 421/454/A. Dunton Green did not gain overall by the arrival of these vehicles, however, as six SMs were transferred out to provide relief at other southeastern garages, primarily Dartford and Swanley. Perhaps more of a surprise was the fact that, some 3½ years after crew duties had ceased, Dunton Green still possessed sufficient conductors to allow for their operation. In the interim these conductors had been loaned to neighbouring garages — mainly Northfleet — on a day-to-day basis to cover staff shortages. They were needed on the MWs as the vehicles did not possess automatic entrance doors, and it was considered impractical for the drivers to operate these manually. The Swifts displaced never returned to Dunton Green, although a handful of the class were used to assist with the removal of the last scheduled RFs in May 1976. The MWs were quite long-lasting however, the final examples not being returned to

Western National until November 1977, despite initial plans that they would go by January 1977, replaced by new SNBs. In reality the latter were used to replace (on paper, at least) the last Swifts. A couple of these lingered on as spare vehicles for a few months, but the last, SM535, moved on to Windsor in April, further new Nationals having provided the necessary replacements.

From this time on, operations at Dunton Green were quite low down my list of interests. All remaining LT influence had gone, and the garage possessed only Nationals and a small number of Bristol LHSs. However, one notable event which occurred some years later, in April 1981, was the return of double-deck operation, using eight of the original 1972 Atlanteans. Coupled with the (by now) normal route restructuring, which occurred simultaneously, the provision of such vehicles was seen as a means of avoiding duplication on many routes which experienced heavy school loadings. An upper deck therefore returned to many services which had made do with single-deck buses since 1972. They also appeared on some routes that had never before featured such a vehicle, and their use through the lanes between Shoreham Village and Sevenoaks on route 404 was startling, to say the least!

Dunton Green garage maintained a considerable number of RFs for its extensive network of predominantly rural services. RF653 stands at Sevenoaks bus station in August 1973 whilst operating on route 454, a service which, in terms of scheduled operation, was then split roughly 50:50 between RF and SM. *Steve Fennell*

Chelsham

ONE location that retained an LT flavour until very late in the day was Chelsham, which was best remembered for its sizeable RT fleet and the large stand and vehicle park that was separate from the main garage structure. Chelsham participated in the great July 1971 OMO programme when it received SMs for its share of the revised 403A service as well as the 453 (Chelsham–Caterham). Those for the 453 entered service prematurely as crew-operated vehicles in May 1971 so as to avoid the need to recertify RT types. Otherwise, Chelsham was predominantly an RT and RF garage and remained so for some considerable time. It was the RFs allocated to the rural 464/465 (Oxted–Westerham/Edenbridge) and 485 (Westerham–Edenbridge) routes that were the first to be removed, when new Bristol LHSs arrived during December 1974. Chelsham nevertheless retained a scheduled RF allocation until October 1975, as problems in accommodating Leyland Nationals had precluded their allocation. Indeed, the Chelsham share of route 706 represented the last regular scheduled use of RFs on Green Line work in the company. The usual appalling availability of the resident Swift fleet also guaranteed regular one-off allocations of RFs, and this would persist until November 1978, more of which anon.

Further Nationals saw off the majority of the small SM fleet in March 1976, but two Swifts remained (albeit one unlicensed), as a full quota of replacements was initially unavailable. The last serviceable SM moved away just one month later, whilst the very last — delicensed SM513 — made its way to Dunton Green in July.

Double-deck operations remained solidly RT until April 1976, when the first Routemaster arrived to commence replacement. Little effect on the overall level of crew work occurred as a result of the 408/470 OMO conversion in June 1972, as London Country had decided that the Croydon–Chelsham corridor was not yet ready to benefit from the full effects of double-deck OMO. Thus Chelsham's predominant operation became the 403 (Wallington–Croydon–Chelsham–Warlingham Park Hospital), with a peak-hour express variation between Chelsham and Croydon.

Chelsham's first Routemaster, RMC1471, arrived in April 1976, and by the following January 10 examples were in residence. Over the ensuing four years Chelsham operated a total of 53 different Routemasters — a staggering figure, considering that the total scheduled crew-bus requirement never exceeded 15 — due to the usual problems posed by CoF expiry and subsequent shortages at other garages.

Even at this time, a shortfall had been predicted for the spring of 1977, and further options were being explored as to how best to address the problem. The logical solution was yet further hired vehicles, and these took the form of a batch of Maidstone Borough Leyland Atlanteans which duly arrived to assist in March 1977. They remained at Chelsham until October, when sufficient Routemasters, by now RCLs, were once again available to allow their return. At one stage, consideration was given

to purchasing them, and one example was subsequently trialled for a few days at Godstone. It failed to impress, however, and, for whatever reason, the purchasing option was not followed through; they returned to Maidstone in November, having last seen service the previous month.

A far more surprising means of tackling the short-term crew-bus shortage was the recertification of a small number of RTs. Four vehicles were chosen, although only three would see service at Chelsham. RT1018, RT3461 and RT604 appeared resplendent in NBC leaf green in April, May and June 1977 respectively. The fourth example, RT981, retained traditional Lincoln green and re-entered service at Reigate in May. Unfortunately the image was spoiled somewhat by their makeshift destination-blind arrangements, proper RT blinds being unavailable, but at least RT604 (and Reigate's RT981) managed to muster a full set. Sadly the RT renaissance was somewhat short-lived; sufficient Routemasters were now becoming available thanks to OMO conversions elsewhere, and a dire shortage of training buses meant that RT1018 and RT3461 were relegated to trainers in September. When RT981 was similarly demoted at Reigate the following February, RT604 became the last survivor in passenger service and continued thus until September 1978, when engine failure brought its precarious existence to an end. Despite intentions to source a replacement, this was not to be, and the bus was sold, fortunately for preservation, the following June. The RT class thus passed from the fleet without ceremony, although a few remained on training duties for just over two years. The very last RT trainer turned out to be RT1018, which was finally withdrawn and sold, again for preservation, in March 1981.

Chelsham was also a very late player in the RF stakes. Two examples were selected for recertification, of which RF221 saw service from Chelsham between September and November 1978. Again, engine failure ultimately brought about its demise, and, with no option of a replacement, it was sold in May 1980.

By May 1977 the 403 'paper' allocation was wholly RMC, although in practice the recertified RTs and Maidstone Atlanteans were covering for non-existent Routemasters. The same month saw the arrival of Chelsham's first RCLs, and throughout the year there arrived steady stream of these vehicles, which eventually replaced not only the hired Atlanteans but also CoF-expired RMCs and two out of the three recertified RTs. By July the 403 allocation had now officially become RCL, but, in reality, vehicle variety was greater than ever! The situation had stabilised by November, when the hired Atlanteans were returned, but four RMCs remained in addition to the sole surviving RT.

From the summer of 1978, as part of a seemingly never-ending saga of vehicle allocations, RMCs once again became the majority type at Chelsham, as CoFs on the RCLs started to expire; RCL2257 was the last of its class to operate on the 403, in December, after which the crew operation at Chelsham was (officially) solely in the hands of RMCs. However, further change was forthcoming, as in October the first new Leyland Atlantean arrived. Due to delivery problems further examples were delayed until the New Year, and OMO conversion of the 403 was deferred from January to March 1979. It was not until February that further Atlanteans arrived, entering service as crew vehicles to replace RMCs, which themselves were now suffering CoF expiry. Full OMO conversion occurred from 3 March, but a small proportion of crew work remained, principally the 403 Express service and, in a surprising role-reversal, the vast majority of the off-peak service on the 453; this was brought about by the need to balance the remaining crew rosters, which also saw a limited amount of off-peak crew work on the 403. A handful of RMCs remained for this remnant of crew operation, although inevitably the odd crew Atlantean would appear.

Further Atlanteans became available towards the end of 1979, and the following February 1980 saw the official conversion of the remaining RMC workings to AN, albeit still retaining conductors. As was the case elsewhere, the last few weeks of Routemaster operation provided a surprise in the form

of two RMLs rendered surplus at Northfleet; CoF expiry had reduced Chelsham's operational RMC fleet to just two examples — RMC1511/5 — by January, and RML2445/52 appeared really as a stop-gap measure to see through the last few weeks of Routemaster operation. RML2452 last worked on 7 February but was replaced by RML2445, which had arrived originally for storage but was pressed into service. Both RMLs saw little use, the usual problems of inoperative heaters and open platforms no doubt having some bearing on the situation, and RML2445, along with the two remaining RMCs, last saw service on 13 February. Surprisingly, conductor operation at Chelsham survived a further six months, until the following August, when the remaining work on the 403, 403 Express and 453 succumbed to the inevitable.

A long-standing RT operation was that of the service between Wallington and Warlingham Park Hospital, latterly numbered 403 in London Country days. In 1973 the future of the route as an RT stronghold was in no doubt and RT4738 is seen approaching Chelsham garage. *Steve Fennell*

Above: The original intention had been to replace Chelsham's RTs with a batch of Bristol VRTs, but a change of plan saw the latter diverted to Grays, and Chelsham was allocated Routemasters. New Atlanteans finally provided an OMO solution for the 403 service, but a small proportion of crew work was retained, primarily for the peak-hour 403 Express service and some off-peak trips on route 453. There had always been one or two crew workings on this route since OMO conversion in July 1971, but the last few months of Routemaster operation saw practically the entire off-peak service reconverted, as spare time existed in the crew rota. RMC1511, seen at Caterham station in July 1979, survived to become one of the last two examples of its type to see service at Chelsham, not being withdrawn until February 1980. *Steve Fennell*

Below: The Croydon–Tonbridge section of route 403 was an early convert in London Country days to the delights of OMO. The newly converted section of route was numbered 403A and in time would be further renumbered 483 to facilitate the introduction of vehicles with three-track number blinds. SM510 stands opposite the large parking area at Chelsham garage in July 1973. *Steve Fennell*

Above: Vehicle shortages dictated that a small number of RTs be recertified during the spring of 1977. RT604, illustrated at West Croydon shortly after recertification in June 1977, found fame as the last of its type to see passenger service with London Country, being finally withdrawn following engine failure in September 1978. Plans to effect a repair did not come to fruition, and the vehicle was sold for preservation a few months later, thus evading any form of official send-off for what was without doubt a significant vehicle type in Country Bus history. *Steve Fennell*